DECREE AND DESTINY

Shaykh Fadhlalla Haeri is a writer-philosopher who combines knowledge and experience of the spiritual teachings of the East with a keen understanding of the West. He was born in Kerbala, Iraq, a descendant of several generations of revered spiritual leaders. Shaykh Fadhlalla's professional experience was primarily as a consultant in industry and business, before embarking upon extensive travelling and teaching.

DECREE
AND
DESTINY

Shaykh Fadhlalla Haeri

Foreword by
Seyyed Hossein Nasr

ELEMENT BOOKS
in association with
ZAHRA PUBLICATIONS

First published in Great Britain in 1991 by
Element Books Limited
Longmead, Shaftesbury, Dorset

Typeset by Crescent Graphics (Pvt) Ltd, Karachi

Printed and bound in Great Britain by
Billings Ltd, Hylton Road, Worcester
Cover design by Max Fairbrother
Front cover painting courtesy of
The Bridgeman Art Library

British Library Cataloguing in Publication Data
Haeri, Fadhlalla
Decree and destiny.
1. Islam
I. Title
297.22

ISBN 1–85230–178–3

Contents

Foreword   xi

Preface   xv

Introduction   xvii

Historical Background   xxi

CHAPTER 1
DECREE AND DESTINY IN THE QUR'AN   1

Qadar and *Qada'* in Language
A Definition of Decree and Destiny
God, the Originator of All
Man's True Impotence
The Inevitability of Death
The Knowledge of the Outcome of Destiny
The Ultimate Dependence
All Creation's Dependence upon the Creator
The Ultimate Record
Man's Freedom within God's Order
Measure and Bounds

Fixed and Changeable Decrees
Man's Unification with the Decree
The Qur'an, the Overall Knowledge
Reality Guides to Itself, by Itself
Heedlessness
The Excuses of the Prevaricators
    and the Role of the Prophets
The Prophet as Transmitter of the Ways of Reality
The Gift of Discrimination
Why Diversity and Duality
Why Some People Cause Themselves Injustice
The Disconnected Ones
Ten Modes of *Qada'* as revealed in the Qur'an
Summary

CHAPTER 2
AFFLICTION, THE ULTIMATE REMEMDY   26

CHAPTER 3
SAYINGS OF THE BLESSED PROPHET   36
AND THE HOLY IMAMS

Introduction
Creation and the Command of God
The Origin of Good and Evil
Compulsion and Delegation
An Injunction of Jurisprudence
Will and Power
The Extent of the Capability of the Bondsman
The Interrelationship between Decree, Action
    and Destiny
God's Covenant with Man
Knowledge of the Decree
The Nature of Action
Contentment with the Decree

Contents

Man's *Rizq*
The Finality of God's Decree
The Purpose of Creation
Decree and Destiny, the Secret of God

CHAPTER 4
SELECTED TOPICS RELATING TO   81
DECREE AND DESTINY

Introduction
Determinism
Certainty and Change
Cause and Effect
Choice within Bounds
    The More the Knowledge, the Less the Choice
    Freedom within the Decree
    The Importance of Gratitude
    Man's Interaction with the Decree
    Knowledge of the Limits
    Man's Choice
    Disappointment or Punishment, an Indicator of
       Wrong or Inappropriate Action
    The Freedom of No Choice
Collective Destiny
Revealed and Acquired Knowledge
The Law of Opposites
Justice
Reward and Punishment
There is no Rule without an Exception
Miracles
Kismet (*Qisma*) — Luck, Fortune
Supplication and Prayer
Causality and Repentance
The Search for Happiness

Equality and Equity
Why People Differ
Selective Search
Bone of Contention
The Creator and Created
A Better Destiny
The Free Man

CONCLUSION   130

Glossary   131
Bibliography   135
Notes   136

Foreword

Nearly every chapter in the long history of Islamic thought is concerned in one way or another with the question of *al-qada' wa'l-qadar*, decree and destiny, or seen in somewhat of a different perspective, free will and determinism. The earliest Islamic community with its intellectual centres in Basra and Kufa was concerned with three basic theological problems: what is the nature of the Qur'an, who is saved, and how is man's free will and moral responsibility based upon choice related to God's omnipotence and also omniscience? Out of these basically Islamic questions related to the teachings of the Qur'an and *hadith*, there grew the earliest schools of theology, or *Kalam*, while the Sufis and the philosophers were also concerned with such questions, especially that of decree and destiny from the earliest times as seen in the utterances of one of the first patriarchs of Sufism, Hasan al-Basri, and the writings of the first Muslim philosophers, such as al-Kindi.

The Qur'an speaks explicitly of both the absolute power and knowledge of God concerning everything in His creation and man's responsibility for his actions, hence his freedom to choose. The *hadith*, which is the supreme commentary upon the Sacred Text, elucidates these teachings by providing additional knowledge concerning a problem which is insoluble upon the plane of rationalistic analysis and without consideration of that inner dimension of the revelation which provides for man's knowledge of the higher levels of existence and of the relativity of man's existence and will vis-a-vis God, who alone is ultimately real.

On the basis of the revealed sources of Islam, numerous responses were to be provided by various schools of thought concerning decree and destiny, free will and determinism. Nearly every Sunni as well as Shi'ite theologian has been concerned with it and in fact the main schools of Sunni *Kalam*, the Ash'ariyyah, Mu'tazilah and Maturidiyyah, have been distinguished from each other mostly on the basis of their attitude towards this question. Likewise, nearly every Islamic philosopher has written on the subject and the separate treatises on decree and destiny by Ibn Sina and Sadr al-Din Shirazi, who came six centuries after him, are well known to students of Islamic thought. As for the Sufis, from the early discourses of Hasan al-Basri and Junayd to the elaborate treatises of 'Abd al-Wahhab al-Sha'rani and 'Abd al-Rahman Jami nearly a millenium later, concern with the question of decree and destiny has remained central. Likewise, one finds this theme pervading the *Mathnawi* of Jalal al-Din Rumi, who has provided some of the most profound answers to this central question of human existence.

In Shi'ism the sayings of the Imams as well as the thought inspired by them provided a rich treasury of wisdom dealing with this theme, a treasury which is much less known to the West than the other sources and modes of Islamic thought. Many sayings of the Imams, especially 'Ali ibn Abi Talib, concern this subject and provide a solution for it at the highest level of metaphysical understanding.

Usually this problem is approached by conceiving of both God and man as 'absolute' realities with 'absolute' wills. Then the question is asked as to how it is possible for God to be omnipotent and omniscient and yet for man to have free will and act according to this freedom. As long as the question is posed in such a way, there is no solution for the dichotomy that it presents to the human mind, and one is faced with the choice of either accepting God's omnipotence and denying human free will or accepting man's free will and denying God's omnipotence, solutions which stand opposed to the very text of the Qur'an as well as the intention of its teachings.

From the point of view of Islamic wisdom or gnosis (*al-hikmah* and *al-ma'rifah*), which is none other than pure metaphysics as expounded through the revealed forms of Islam on the basis of the inner dimensions of the Islamic revelation, only God is absolute while man is relative. Moreover, according to the *hadith, khalaqa'Llahu Adama 'ala suratihi* (God has created man upon His 'form'), man reflects God's Names and Qualities which constitute the *surah* referred to in this *hadith*. Now, it must be remembered that God is both pure necessity and pure freedom; therefore, something of both qualities have to be reflected in man. Man is determined by God through all the conditions of existentiation which make him be what he is, but he is also free to 'unbecome' what he is through ascending the grades and scales of existence towards the one who alone is pure freedom. Man's will, moreover, is free in the ultimate sense only in conforming itself to the Will of God. We are free to the degree that we *are*, to the degree that we approach the One who alone *is* in the absolute sense. Man is what he becomes and becomes what he is because his actions affect his existence while his existence determines the modes of his actions. He is determined because God is pure necessity and the source of all existence; he is free because he is the mirror in which are reflected the Divine Qualities and Attributes including freedom which is concomitant of His absoluteness. Human existence is that great mystery woven of the warp of necessity and the woof of freedom. That is why man alone is the microcosm, the key to universal existence and the only being who while himself, can go beyond himself, who is bound yet free, who realizes real freedom through surrendering his will to God and who realizes pure necessity by making use of his God-given freedom to become what he is in the Divine Presence.

Shaykh Fadhlalla Haeri's book has the great advantage that it presents to the Western reader the deepest aspects of the problems of decree and destiny through the actual words of the Qur'an, the Prophet and the Shi'ite Imams. Many of the sayings translated in this work, especially those of the Imams, have not been available in such a manner before in their direct relation to the intricacies of the question of *qada'* and *qadar*. His work does not attempt to be a complete theological or philosophical treatment of the subject. Rather, he draws from the traditional sources numerous sayings, complemented by his own commentaries, to present to the reader the remarkable richness of Islamic thought on this issue and to remove some of the well-known errors concerning Islam such as Islam being fatalistic and having no room for human initiative and dynamism, as if early Islam did not spread from China to France in a century or it did not create one of the greatest civilizations in human history.

Shaykh Fadhlalla Haeri must be congratulated on making the deepest sources of Islamic thought concerning the question of decree and destiny available to the Western and also modern Muslim reader who often relies upon works in English or French even concerning Islamic subjects. May this work help dispel that cloud of ignorance which surrounds this central issue of human existence. May those destined to profit from the sources of Islamic thought presented in this work, be decreed to benefit fully from it through the freedom of the use of their intelligence which God has bestowed upon all human beings as His supreme gift.

Seyyed Hossein Nasr
Washington, D.C.
Shawwal 1407 (A.H.)
June 1987 (A.D.)

Preface

The principal objective of this book is to establish a bridge between the Islamic cultures and philosphies and the West, and to
encourage westerners to draw upon this most recent among all
revivals of the Eternal Truth, use the knowledge they acquire
from its study, and integrate it into their own system, instead of
regarding it as an eastern curiosity or an object of study for the
sake of scholarly achievement, as has been the case with most
of the orientalists of both western and eastern origin. Prophetic
knowledge is not the preserve of any nation or culture, for it is
Reality's gift to all creation.

This highly condensed book will be of most use if it is taken
as one building block from among several complementary units
that the author hopes to bring out. This series of publications
relating to broad themes such as decree and destiny, personal
psychology and cosmology, all dovetail into each other.

As 'Decree and Destiny' has largely been compiled as a usable
manual for the English speaking reader, the quotations from the
Qur'an and *hadith* (tradition, saying, of the Blessed Prophet and
the Holy Imams) are those that would be easily comprehended
by the western mind. All the traditions cited are, with few exceptions, those which have been related by the Holy Imams of the
Ahl al-Bayt (Household of the Blessed Prophet). We firmly believe
that without the assistance of these traditions it would not be
possible to present a full picture of the question of decree and
destiny. In addition, they are those which will be most helpful
in dispelling the inaccurate picture many non-Muslims have of

Islam as a fatalistic religion.

As this is a multi-dimensional topic, apparent repetitions have been left in the text in order to bring about the proper merging of various interrelated facts. The recurrence of similar themes is like the emergence of a pattern in a mosaic or threads in a tapestry where the use of the same tile pattern or colour of thread complements another pattern and holds the total design together. As the concepts that we have tried to cover in this book deal with varying aspects of existence and reality, identical topics will appear in different dimensions. Thus the same grain of truth will support different theories in a multi-faceted panorama.

The nature of Reality has so many dimensions, and each dimension itself integrates and interlinks with other discoveries in an ever-changing spectrum. Thus the knowledge of Reality cannot be disseminated by controlled scientific methods. The seeker has to move from one dimension to another, exploring their different facets, until the entire model begins to take shape subjectively in time. One starts from logic and reason and ends with insight and awakening, hence each voyage of discovery has its own unique flavour. At the best the reader will share some of the subjective experiences of the commentator and, guided by the beams of light he has gleaned from these insights, he will make his own ascent up the mountains of discovery.

He must cross many of these mountains if he is to get the picture of the entire ridge. On his journey he will traverse many valleys and ravines, which are cloaked in darkness. It is only when he gains the total picture of Reality experientially and feels the unifying power of the timeless Source that these gaps will begin to disappear; for it is impossible to fill them by prescriptive, scientific methods.

While the writer does not expect a single reader to emerge content and satisfied, having integrated himself with the total picture, he hopes there will be some who, having seen further and, embarking on the quest for self-knowledge, evolve according to the unchanging programme of the Absolute Creator.

Introduction

The issue of the extent to which man has free will has been the frequent topic of philosophical debate from the early civilizations of Egypt and Greece right through to our own times, while western philosophers such as Spinoza, Descartes, Leibnitz and Kant, to name but a few of the most noted, have added their interpretations to the theories of the ancients. Equally it is a most subtle and important topic in the study of Islamic thought, for it cannot be understood by pure philosophical, analytical or spiritual debate. It has to be based on theory and practice for it to be fully comprehended, as it requires both subtle inner understanding as well as gross experiential realization. For this reason it has been misunderstood throughout the ages.

There are two distinguishable problems under discussion. One is the relationship between the will of God and man's will, the other is the relationship between God's power and His overall control.

A large body of verses from the Qur'an and many traditions in the Islamic heritage deal with these issues. This book contains a selection of what the writer believes to be the most significant and illuminating on the subject of decree and destiny.

All of us face situations, within our existential experience, where we have varying degrees of choice. At the same time we are often placed in a position where we appear to be helpless in influencing the outcome of that particular situation. The foundation or the basis that illustrates the reality behind these two different situations is explained in this book. The concept of decree and destiny falls in the interspace between these two possibilities of absolute decree and absolute choice, within which the opposing aspects of 'choice' and 'no-choice', 'freedom' and 'slavery', must be considered.

As we contemplate the meaning of 'freedom', the following questions arise: If there are absolute laws that govern existence, and if these laws are immutable and unchangeable, then how can there be freedom? Why do we blame ourselves if we make mistakes, instead of blaming them on the immutable laws? An apparent dichotomy, however, remains. If there is freedom, and we are free to choose our course of action, where then is the position of the All-Powerful in relation to the laws that govern our actions in this existence?

Such questions have been examined under various headings and by many different schools of thought within Islamic philosophy. As early as the middle of the first century after Hijrah we find two opposing schools of thought emerging in Islam. One, the Jabariyyah (from *jabr*, to enforce), believe that all of us are subject to an unknown and absolute decree, which we cannot in any way overcome or interfere with; the other, the Qadariyyah, say that human beings have complete freedom of choice to decide their own destiny.

The Jabariyyah maintain that God is entirely responsible for the actions of His creatures — the implication being that He forces them to do wrong, then punishes them for it, and forces them to do good, then rewards them for it. It follows, therefore, that the actions of people are really God's actions but are metaphorically attributed to people because human beings are the locus of God's activity. The reason for this hypothesis arises from the Jabariyyah's denial of the existence of natural causes between things, saying that God is the cause; there being no other cause besides Him. The Jabariyyah base their argument for this assumption on the belief that God is the Creator without any partner. However, it should be noted that such a claim on the part of this school's adherents is the equivalent of attributing injustice to God. This point will be examined later in the book.

The Qadariyyah hold the opposite view; namely, that all actions on the part of humans are free and are not predetermined by the will of God. Adherents of this school maintain that God has given full power to His creatures for their actions; as the power is fore-ordained, the decree of God has no part to play in it. The reason they hold this view is that they consider the attribution of man's actions to God necessitates the attributing of imperfection to Him. Their view is that all existing things have specific causes, and that the chain of causes and effects can be traced back to the Cause of causes, the First Cause, which is God. It must be noted, however, that those who adhere to this school of thought have separated God from His power, and have thus given Him partners in His creation. This presents an equally problematic view with regard to the concept of decree and destiny.

Our beliefs, delineated in this book, concerning the position of man in relation both to Divine Decree and to his destiny, follow the teachings of our Blessed Prophet, Muhammad, and his heirs, the Imams. Our central position is one which maintains that the reality of the question raised lies between the two extremes that are depicted by the opposing schools of the Jabariyyah and the Qadariyyah. This view presents a middle may between the two extreme beliefs mentioned in the preceding paragraphs.

Imam Ja'far al-Sadiq points out that, from one point of view, our actions are truly our own actions. According to this reasoning, we are the cause of our own actions, which are under our control and are subject to our free choice. However, from another point of view, our actions are decreed by God and are subject to His power. This is because it is God Who bestows existence. God does not compel us in our actions, hence He does not wrong us by punishing us for our errors; for we have the power of choice in what we do. Yet, God has not delegated to us the power to 'create' our actions, for the overall control remains with Him. Creation, Judgement and Command all belong to God. He has power over all things, and He has complete authority over all people.

Our belief is that determinism and Divine Decree are among the secrets of God. We maintain that those who have understood Divine Decree and destiny, in the way that they should be understood without resorting to either of the two extremes we have mentioned, will have attained true knowledge. We hope to explicate this belief for our readers, God willing.

As we examine the philosophical history of Islam, we find that no century has passed without the question of decree and destiny having been raised. Philosophers and gnostics alike have all examined this question deeply. Our belief is that the key to a true understanding of the issue lies in the Sayings of the Imams. It is by examining their Sayings that we plan to unfold the full meaning of what decree is, and how man must realize his own destiny in the world in which he lives.

The traditions related from our first Imam, 'Ali ibn Abi Talib, are the most helpful we have seen in human communication regarding the topic of decree and destiny. We consider that other sources we have examined do not yield the full fruit of the knowledge we seek. The utterances of the Sufis are generally of little assistance for they do not provide us with the key to unlock the complete meaning of decree and destiny. Although we have gleaned from some of these utterances that there have been Sufis who have known the truth, we have equally recognized the existence of a barrier which Sufi literature has not penetrated.

In our present book we shall first examine the Holy Qur'an, so as to enable the reader to become familiar with the philosophical foundations of what has been said regarding this issue; second, we shall turn to the Sayings of the Blessed Prophet and the Holy Imams for further clarification.

This important subject of decree and destiny is the least understood of similar fundamental issues that pertain to the position of man in relation to Reality. The source of the knowledge of this subject is beyond language, beyond mere words and forms, and if one really wants to tap the source, one must die to oneself. One's being must be annihiliated in the True Being, the Transcendent, the One God.

Historical Background

During the early days of Islam, the light of the presence of the Blessed Prophet was such that an understanding of the laws of existence and man's freedom within these bounds was transmitted to the people. However, with the confusions and difficulties that followed his death there was, in a sense, a break in that light, and the question of free will and predestination became a much debated issue.

The Umayyad dynasty used theological arguments to justify their rule, declaring that God predetermines all happenings and acts. Their possession of the Caliphate was therefore by God's will, and the people were consequently obliged to submit to their rule. Their political opponents took the opposing stance that while good actions are from God, base actions are from man, so no blame can be attributed to God as He has delegated freedom of action to man.

The name 'Qadarite' was commonly used to describe those who denied the *qadar* or predetermination of God, and were thus believers in human free will. At a later date, it was also used in a negative way to describe those of a fatalistic persuasion. The founder of this school of thought is generally considered to be Ma'bad al-Juhani. He denied that the wrong acts of the Umayyads were determined by God. He joined the rising of Ibn al-Ash'ath in 701 AD, for which he was subsequently executed. Another noted exponent of the Qadarite school was Ghaylan ad-Dimashqi, a Copt, who also rebelled against the Umayyads and was executed. It is claimed that the Caliph Yazid III al-

Naqis, who reigned for some months in 774 AD, was a follower of Ghaylan. The Caliph certainly stated that the Umayyads had committed wrong actions and pledged himself to correct them, and to rule according to the Qur'an and the *Sunnah* (way, habitual custom, line of conduct; used in preference to God or the Blessed Prophet).

The Jabariyyah concept of predestination was indigenous to the areas where Islam first arose, where people tended to hold fatalistic beliefs. The pre-Islamic poetry of Arabia is full of references to the control of human life by 'time', which was seen as an abstract, impersonal force. This concept acted as a psychological necessity for the nomad, releasing him from undue anxiety about events he was unable to control, and adapting him to acceptance of extreme irregularities of even natural phenomena, such as rain. The Arabian nomad believed that it was the outcome of man's acts that were fixed, not the particular acts themselves. They believed that the day of his death was fixed, as was his *rizq* (provision), which was a comforting thought in a land where hunger was prevalent.

The Qur'an revealed man's life to be controlled by a merciful God, rather than the impersonal and unfeeling Time. The doctrine of a final Day of Judgement confirmed the eternal destiny of man, which was to be determined by the quality of his actions.

The people's acquiescence in the abuses of the Umayyad rule can thus be understood as the natural continuation of the pre-Islamic Arab outlook. The Umayyad argument, that as they were the Caliphs or Deputies of God everything they did was decreed by God, including their evil actions, was in harmony with the fatalistic heritage of many of the people they ruled. Nonetheless, it would be over-simplistic to conclude that theological argument was the prime contributor to the survival of the dynasty, power and coercion being equally significant factors.

The Qadariyyah stance that good acts emanate from God, the bad from man, was similar to the principles of Christianity and like Christianity showed clear traces of Hellenistic rationalism. Many proponents of this belief may have been recent converts from Christianity, and may also have come from urban rather than from nomadic backgrounds.

It is clear that a diverse range of views were held by people under the umbrella of Qadariyyah. The more extreme held that total power had been delegated to man, hence he was able to act without God's help and guidance, but others will have had more moderate beliefs. The great Sufi Master, Hasan al-Basri, who was considered to have Qadarite sympathies, for example, rejected a fully deterministic outlook, and preached that a belief in predestination should not be used for inactivity. He emphasized individual responsibility in the moral sphere, but balanced this by insistence on God's mercy, and His ultimate control of man's destiny.

These varying interpretations of the extent of man's free will were later refined by the philosophers of the Mu'tazilite school, who were to develop the doctrines of the Qadariyyah. Their founder, Wasil ibn 'Ata' (80–131 AH/699–749 AD), was originally a member of the circle of Hasan al-Basri. By the ninth century AD the Qadariyyah school had been largely replaced by the Mu'tazilite. The latter were engaged in endless debate with the Ash'arites, so named after their founder Abu al-Hasan al-Ash'ari (d 330 AH/942 AD), in an attempt to find a balance between the omnipotence of God and the need for personal moral effort.

The Ash'arites, could be regarded to some extent as being the successors of the Jabariyyah; Abu al-Hasan al-Ash'ari himself was originally a pupil of the Mu'tazilite Master, al-Jubba'i. He broke from his teacher in maintaining that Divine Justice could not be defined in human terms, and was in agreement with the orthodox stance as expounded by Ahmad ibn Hanbal (d 241 AH/855 AD) by which all acts, be they good or evil, take place by the will of God; as compared to the Mu'tazilite theories, which appear to restrict the power of God.

One of al-Ash'ari's contemporaries was Abu Mansur al-Maturidi (d 333 AH/945 AD) of Samarqand. Maturidism, which is similar to Ash'arism in basic outlook, differs in saying that although all acts are willed by God, evil acts do not occur with 'the good pleasure of God'. This theory emphasizes the omnipotence of God but allows for some human participation in the process.

The more extreme among the Jabariyyah were sometimes referred to as Jahmiyyah, from the name of Jahm ibn Safwan, who was purported to have upheld the theory of pure determinism. In actuality this was more a term of abuse used by members of the opposing schools to link the Jabariyyah with a known historical character of the period, who was regarded as a renegade. He had fought with a non-Muslim Turkish Sultan against his fellow Muslims. There was never any serious group who were followers of this man or preached his teachings.

As many of the Qadariyyah were motivated by their political opposition to the Umayyads, the rise to power of the Abbasids altered the relationship of this doctrine to the political situation of the day. It was no longer seen as a sign of opposition to the government. Indeed, the Caliph al-Ma'mun and his successors gave official backing to certain Mu'tazilite doctrines. However, after the Caliph Mutawakkil the question of *jabr* once more rose to prominence. This was partly caused by a reaction against the excesses of the extreme Mu'tazilites, who were branded as heretics by the orthodox Muslims, but it was also brought about by the appeal this belief has for man, when his state seems helpless. Indeed as a philosophy it possessed a great deal of political advantage, because it persuaded people to submit even to despotic rulership. Thus a belief in decree and destiny in its goodness and its badness was frequently twisted to cow people into an acceptance of unjust government.

The advocates of determinism often used the example that man is like a leaf in the wind of destiny, and that God creates in man his actions and all his doings in the same way that He does in stones and other forms of His creation. So man does not have the power to change or do anything. They used selected *ayat* (verses) of the Qur'an and traditions to justify this hypothesis; indeed if one looks at many of these in a simplistic fashion, the theory holds.

Generally speaking the majority of the Sunni oriented Muslim population veered towards the Ash'ariyyah school of thought;

while the Shi'as and some Sunnis argued for a more intermediate position, which allowed for the existence of a certain measure of freedom in specific areas, while in other aspects man has no choice. So these divisions are in a sense simplistic, and historians, who like to compartmentalize, have often tended to show the extremes of the argument, while the majority of the believing Muslim population will have fallen between the two positions, without necessarily having total clarity of understanding of the extent of man's freedom of action or the bounds to which he is subjected.

The widespread influence of the Ash'ariyyah can be seen in all Arabic, Persian and Far Eastern literature and poetry. Their influence is even reflected in the culture of the Ja'fari Shi'as. It is largely due to this that many European philosophers and men of literature, casting a cursory glance at the broad spectrum of Muslim attitudes on predestination, have labelled them as fatalistic. Indeed one of the major criticisms and miscomprehensions of Islam by non-Muslims and also by some so-called Muslims is focused on the question of decree and destiny. The accusation is that one of the main causes for the backwardness of some Muslim communities is their belief in predestination. If belief in the knowledge of decree and destiny is a cause of lethargy and inactivity, with the subsequent decadence and collapse of the culture, how then can we explain the many great Islamic effulgences of the past fourteen hundred years?

Acknowledgements

The author would like to acknowledge the help of all who assisted in the preparation of this book, in particular Muneera Haeri for editing it, Abdul Razaq Sheriff, Batul Haeri and Dr. A. Hashemian who also contributed to the preparation of transcripts and formatting of the text, and Muna H. Bilgrami for correcting the translation and proofing.

1

Decree and Destiny in the Qur'an

Qadar (decree) and *Qada'* (destiny) in Language

In language *qadar* (measure, decree) represents both the delineation and execution of the process by which a final end, signified by *qada'* (destiny) is arrived at. The connotation of processing attached to *qadar* contains within it the possibility of change; whereas, when a destiny (*qada'*) has come about a point of irreversibility has been reached.

The divine meaning of *qadar* signifies 'creational decree', while its human meaning implies 'judgement by word or action'. There is a clear differentiation between Divine *Qudrah* (ability, power) and human *qudrah*, for human ability differs according to the magnitude of the task, the effort and power it needs to be executed, and is subject to time, whereas for the absolute Creator all actions are possible and effortless at all times.

The following are some of the dictionary definitions of *qadar* and *qada'*:

> *Qadar*: 'extent, scope, quantity, scale, rate, measure, number, sum, amount, degree, grade, worth, value, standing, rank, Divine Decree'. *Qadar* can also imply 'clarifying, distinguishing, ordering, ordaining'.
> *Qada'*: 'severing, ending, closing; determination, conclusion, winding up, completion, accomplishment, carrying out, execution, performance, fulfillment, satisfaction, payment, passing, Divine Decree, destiny, fate, judgement'.

1

A Definition of Decree and Destiny

Decrees are the rules of this game of life. Most of these rules are describable or measurable, especially those dealing with the visible realities. The rules that govern all aspects of physical (visible and experiential) existence combine with those that control the unseen forces to form a network that will result in, for example, the laws of physics. We can describe the phenomenon of light, for instance, as both a waveband and a physical entity called a photon. The rules somehow emerge from an unknown ocean into describable, measurable, physical laws. So the decrees can be seen as a series of multitudinal models by means of which the creation, seen and unseen, is held together. They are abstract and absolute — pure electric power to which man adds his actions.

Destiny is the final judgement (occurrence) that is experienced by the individual through the passage of time, when these laws are enacted. It is when a describable, measurable event has already passed through time.

The concept of destiny is also parallel in Arabic to another term *ajal*, which signifies 'appointed time, date, deadline, instant of death, respite, delay'. If we say a business partnership has an '*ajal*' of five years, it means that at the end of this period it will have reached its full destiny, which is dissolution.

The final destiny of every man is his awakening to his permanent non-time reality, from which he has emerged. We are given the experience of this life, with all its decrees, for us to know them, accept them and become one with them so that we can see our destiny within them, and our destiny beyond them, when time stops at the point of death.

We have been given the ability, if we use meditative practices, to stop time inwardly, and experience a form of mini-death while we are still alive. This enables us to experience aspects of full death, which is our final destiny, as free will. We are programmed to fear the unknown so we are afraid of death. However, on the other hand, we love and are dependent on deep sleep, which is

2

the nearest experience to death. If we are able to experience the mini-death of inner contemplation, we stand a good chance of realizing that our true reality, the Source of the cause behind existence, is eternal. It is only the body that dies, while the self continues into perpetuity.

As we are all programmed to dislike fear, the universal fear of death betrays the true meaning of death. It is only an experiential barrier that demarcates a natural discrimination by returning the body to where it belongs, and by returning the soul or real self to whence it originally emanated in the zone of eternal consciousness. So the fact that we do not like death reveals a certain measure of its falsehood. Death does have its reality but this reality has its segregations. Thus the real problem is that of confusion; we have identified our *nafs* (self, soul, mind) with the body. Our reasoning ensures that we will die, yet it is only the body that dies; for it has been the vehicle for the development of the self, and its proper schooling lies in the melting pot of the world of duality, whilst yearning for the knowledge of the One from Whom it emanated in the first place.

It will be unveiled to us that our ultimate destiny is the highest of destinies, as our beginning was the highest of beginnings. We were brought into the lowest level of existence with its laws so we might be prepared for access to the highest. So destiny is at all levels and at all times. Our physical destiny is death, yet we can experience a spiritual death (disconnection) while still alive.

Our destiny is also to know the perfection and reliability of God's creational will; a greater recognition of the flimsiness of man's free will helps us to achieve this objective. Once this recognition of no choice is reached, a point of complete abandonment will come, until we see nothing other than the abundance that is available at all times to everyone. This is the final awakening to the state of oneness. We are brought into time in order that we may face the incredible, unfathomable, foreverness of non-time. So we are already predestined to face endless time. If we veer against this destiny, we have cut across the decree and the decree will cut us.

3

An examination of the following collection of Qur'anic *ayat* (plural of *ayah*: Qur'anic verse; sign or mark) concerning decree and destiny will bring out the various senses and concomitant modes of the concepts we are studying.

We will begin with some key *ayat* on this topic, then move to other *ayat*, which further clarify the purpose of the Creator and the role of His creation.

God, the Originator of All

> They entertained about Allah thoughts of ignorance quite unjustly, saying: We have no hand in the affair. Say: Surely the affair is wholly (in the hands) of Allah.
>
> (3:154)

The Qur'an confirms that all creational possibilities, and therefore all experiences, emanate originally from God. However, we are only acting out of ignorance and attempting to avoid personal responsibility when we attribute blame to God in situations where we have not exposed and exerted ourselves sincerely. God's will is that good prevails, and that man gears himself towards the positive in order to increase his knowledge of discrimination and awareness. Only the hypocrite sits idly by, and says: "God wills". This will happen automatically, even though his negative stance challenges, in one sense, God's will, and the thought itself indicates separateness and loss.

Whenever beings or nations have cut across natural laws, they have eventually been destroyed. The story of the people of the Prophet Lut (Lot) — the Biblical Sodom and Gomorrah — with their homosexuality is an example of this. These events stand as a lesson to those who are alive, in order that they may reflect and discover the right path of action for every occurrence. Whatever is in this cosmos, be it energy or matter, small or large, is subject to the laws that govern the entirety. We must be prepared to recognize the bounds of these laws and their interactions, which are operative at all times, and know the outcome.

Man's True Impotence

> And certainly we have already destroyed the likes of you,
> but is there anyone who will mind?
> And everything they have done is in the writings.
> And everything small and great is written down.
>
> (54:51–3)

The implication here is of the impotence of man. He has no power over that which matters most — destiny. All his actions and their outcomes are recorded in the heavenly books, and every cell of his body is a microcosm of the entire heavens. Everything, be it small or large, is accounted for. Nothing escapes the laws, and a small thing out of balance in these multitudinal laws can disturb the entire ecology.

Although we may have a measure of interaction and influence on the worlds within and without us, we are truly impotent as far as the purpose of our creation is concerned. We were created to know the original love of the Creator, with Whom we were before creation, with Whom we are during the experience of existence, and with Whom we will be forever. So our impotence is total where it matters. Once that total impotence is recognized, the freedom of surrender will be chosen. That surrender is Islam.

The Inevitability of Death

> And a soul will not die but with the permission of Allah;
> the term is fixed; and whoever desires the reward of this
> world, I shall give him of it, and whoever desires the
> reward of the hereafter I shall give him of it; and I will
> reward the grateful.
>
> (3:145)

Death is an experience that every self will go through according to the unfolding of time and its destiny. No one can escape death, though its specific occurrence in time is usually unknown to man. The freedom man has lies in relation to his achieving desired objectives. If they are worldly and material, he is likely to get

5

them. The person who is in a state of gratitude, and thereby less agitated and concerned, is more likely to succeed whether the objective is material or spiritual.

The Knowledge of the Outcome of Destiny

> He it is Who created you from clay, then He decreed a term. And there is a term named after Him; still you doubt.
>
> (6:2)

Every destiny is known in the non-time dimension but, for us who are in time, the particular and circumstantial outcome is not known. Man's destiny is known to God, for God is beyond time and space. Man, however, can play a crucial role in that destiny and make changes within the prescribed limitations that have been ordained for Him.

The same issue is referred to, in the communal sense, in:

> And for every nation there is a term, so when their term is come they shall not remain behind the least while, nor shall they go before.
>
> (7:34)

Every creational phenomenon has a beginning and an end. In the same way that man eventually dies, his community or nation will also reach its end. Sometimes the end of a phenomenon may be postponed, while at other times the course is so firmly set that there is no way of avoiding the final doom. However, all of these destinies are existential and within time frames. What really matters is the destiny and the course, which is timeless, and which occurs after departing from this world. Compared with this fixed destiny, other destinies become so insignificant. It is in this respect that the believer is exhorted to prepare himself and be ready for the next life.

The Ultimate Dependence

> Say: I do not control for myself any harm, nor any benefit

except what Allah pleases. Every nation has a term. When
their term comes, they shall not then remain for an hour,
nor can they go before.

(10:49)

This *ayah* indicates that man cannot interfere with destiny or
the decree. We do not possess for ourselves either harm or goodness unless God has willed it. We can see potentially what is
harmful to us, and what is beneficial, if we abandon our will
into God's will, Who is the All-Merciful, the All-Beneficent.
Everything that is harmful comes from associating other than
God with God and denying His reality.

If we see the one and only Reality, we do not see two. We
will not see the outer event happening, and worry whether that
which we desire or expect will clash with it. If we have no wishes,
how can we be harmed? We cannot change events. Even the
Blessed Prophet did not have that power. Arrows hit him in the
mouth and made him bleed. The natural laws that propelled
those arrows are irrevocable. All that can change is in accordance
with God's will, and what God wills is the best for His true
slaves. The best they can do is to abandon their will into His.
This is what happens when the Blessed Prophet and any of those
who follow in his footsteps abandon their will to the will of
Reality, accepting that the laws that govern the physical reality
are immutable. Once we do this, we see the beauty of the Divine
laws and accept them contentedly.

There is no doubt, however, that in our relative worldly existence we continuously call upon and depend on ways and means.
The body is made dependent on physical matter — ie, food —
but this is only a means for us to recognize the knowledge that
came about because of these limitations and dependences. Dependence on food and our innate love of freedom propels us to
discover the optimum way of growing food and these processes
increase our network of knowledge of cause and effect.

So on the physical level it is the physical realities that take us
to higher realities for, once the body and its needs are satisfied,
the mind and the intellect seek their satisfaction. We seek inde-

pendence at the physical level and move onward.

The final part is the realization of our dependence on One Reality, which guides us from the beginning to the end, for that Reality encompasses both beginning and end and in Itself is devoid of both.

All Creation's Dependence upon the Creator

> And there is no animal in the earth but on Allah is the sustenance of it, and He knows its resting place and its depository. All (things) are in a manifest book.
>
> (11:6)

There is nothing that moves on the earth except that its provision rests upon reality.

The Ultimate Record

> And those who disbelieve say: The hour shall not come upon us. Say: Yea! By my Lord, the Knower of the unseen, it shall certainly come upon you. Not the weight of an atom becomes absent from Him, in the heavens or in the earth, and neither less than that nor greater, but (all) is in a clear book.
>
> (34:3)

This *ayah* is emphatic that no matter how insignificant something may appear to you, it has its place in the book, and it cannot be escaped — ie, it relates to a clearly defined pattern and presentation.

The following *ayah* is along the same lines.

> And Allah created you from dust, then from the life-germ, then He made you pairs. And no female bears, nor does she bring forth, except with His knowledge. And no one whose life is lengthened has his life lengthened, nor is aught diminished of one's life, but it is all in a book. Surely this is easy for Allah.
>
> (35:11)

Nothing comes to earth nor within ourselves unless it is according to Divine laws. We understand that whatever comes to us outwardly is according to the laws of physiology, biology and anatomy. Equally, we are affected by what we call 'psychological' laws, which interact with the physical ones, although they are more subtle. They exist more at the energy levels and are less easily measurable, because they are not scientifically defined (or reproducible in controlled conditions).

We cannot easily understand the self (*nafs*), and cure its sicknesses, so we tend to dwell too much on the bodily side of our existence. The Science of the Self (Science of the *Nafs*), as practised by the spiritual masters, is ignored and dismissed as unscientific. Yet it follows precise laws, which are clearly set out in the Qur'an.

When the Qur'an says that all of this is written in a book, it means everything is according to the laws that govern existence.

Man's Freedom within God's Order

> And give him sustenance from whence he thinks not. And whoever trusts in Allah, He is sufficient for him. Surely Allah attains His purpose. Allah indeed has appointed a measure for everything.
>
> (65:3)

God's order will prevail; He will attain His decree. There is a measure (decree) for everything, so man's transgressions are according to a measure, and are thus containable.

This aspect is also emphasized in:

> He will forgive you some of your faults and grant you a delay to an appointed term. Surely the term of Allah when it comes is not postponed, did you but know.
>
> (71:4)

When the appointed time of Reality comes, it will never be delayed.

Measure and Bounds

Imam 'Ali al-Rida defined *qadar* as:

> The arrangements (*structuring*) as far as its length and its height and its duration are concerned.

The following collection of *ayat* reflect the Imam's definition:

> And there is not a thing but with Us are the treasures of it, and We do not send it down but in a known measure.
>
> (15:21)

The effect of what manifests into the creational reality can be markedly different from its origin — ie, something subtle can become gross; also what happens to be good under most circumstances can also be bad at other times while its origin of pure consciousness is always neutral.

> He...Who created everything, then ordained for it a measure.
>
> (25:2)

> ...And there is a measure with Him of everything.
>
> (13:8)

> He said: Our Lord is He Who gave to everything its creation, then guided it (to its goal).
>
> (20:50)

The last *ayah* describes how once creation is manifested it is bound by Reality's laws. The resultant physical manifestations are fully discernible, describable, weighable.

> And Who makes (things) according to a measure, then guides (them to their goal).
>
> (87:3)

One of the meanings of the above *ayah* is that God has guided what He has created to what He had intended it or measured it for.

> Of a small seed He created him, then He made him
> according to a measure.
> Then (as for) the way — He has made it easy (for him).
>
> (80:19–20)

These *ayat* show that God makes it easy for man to reach the awakening for which he has been created, but it does not contradict the existence of man's relative freedom within his bounds. In fact, the freedom man is given is for the purpose of discovering the bounds, recognizing their perfection, and choosing to remain within those bounds; for he is programmed to undergo afflictions and punishment whenever he transgresses those bounds and, as he dislikes afflictions, he will naturally choose the path of seeking the knowledge of those bounds and keeping within them.

Fixed and Changeable Decrees

We are shown decree and destiny from the standpoint both of God and man in:

> Say: I do not know whether that with which you are
> threatened be nigh or whether Allah will appoint it for a
> term.
>
> The Knower of the unseen! So He makes His secrets known
> to none.
>
> Except to him whom He chooses as an apostle; for surely
> He makes a guard to march before him and after him,
>
> So that He may know that they have truly delivered the
> messages of their Lord, and He encompasses what is with
> them, and He records the number of all things.
>
> (72:25–8)

11

There are two types of decree; those which are changeable and those which are set. As we can never be sure when it is the final decree, it is essential that we constantly make supplication, by expressing permitted and meritorious desires, and maintaining an attitude of optimism for change. We are calling upon that Mercy to manifest that the final decree has been set; again at its point of finality we expect to experience and witness the Mercy. So the Mercy encompasses all states whether we are desirous of a change, or an event has occurred in spite of our being unable to change it.

The first *ayah* implies that man is an integral element in the process of himself experiencing his destiny. Nobody knows for certain the extent of the individual's interference with his own destiny. The outcome or destiny of every situation is a mixture of the environment, which includes society and all other ecologies, as well as the personal individual action. The total outcome is dependent on all of these forces interacting with each other. As far as matters of personal implication are concerned — eg, closing one's eyes — the individual can exert maximum influence. The more people a situation involves, the less the certainty of the outcome, such as in politics, which involves the opinions and desires of many.

This *ayah*, therefore, can be seen as a dynamic model involving unseen destiny and that destiny which is directly acted upon by the subject himself.

The Prophets, or those highly evolved souls to whom certain revelations occur, are beings of the highest level of submission. Their state is such that on occasions they experience the bridge between the physical 'in time' and the unseen 'non-time', which gives birth to all realities and their destinies. These Messengers of Truth are the interface between the permanent everlasting, all-encompassing Reality, and the changing realities. They are the interlinks between the All-Knower and the relative knower, man. They see the fixed screen upon which the movie of life is projected, and thereby sometimes see the next act before its actual projection.

Man's Unification with the Decree

> So you did not slay them, but it was Allah Who slew
> them, and you did not smite when you smote (the enemy),
> but it was Allah Who smote, and that He might confer
> upon the believers a good gift from himself. Surely Allah
> is Hearing, Knowing.
>
> (8:17)

When man abandons himself totally to the will of God, he becomes the decree itself by giving in totally to the decree and flowing along with events as they manifest themselves. This is the ultimate prayer, when the actor completely takes on the script. Even when the role is difficult he completely identifies with it.

The above *ayah* referring to the Prophet Musa (Moses) is an example of this. The Prophet Moses acted in accordance with the Divine inspiration he received. He himself was astounded by what transpired. His destiny was to be the decree. In his confrontation with the Pharaoh, the decree and he were one. It had been decreed that certain events would take place, and he was a part of these happenings. His action was no longer his action. He abandoned himself entirely into God's will. This is the ultimate celebration of slavehood. When the part connects totally with the whole it manifests the characteristics of the whole. When the bondsman recognizes his real slavehood and fully submits to the Master, he acts in such unity with his Creator that the separation of the two almost disappears.

The Qur'an, the Overall Knowledge

> And even if there were a Qur'an with which the mountains
> were made to pass away, or the earth were travelled over
> with it, or the dead were made to speak thereby. Nay!
> The commandment is wholly Allah's. Have not yet those
> who believe known that if Allah please He would certainly
> guide all the people? And (as for) those who disbelieve,
> there will not cease to afflict them because of what they

13

do a repelling calamity, or it will alight close by their abodes, until the promise of Allah comes about. Surely Allah will not fail in (His) promise.

(13:31)

The Holy Qur'an is the word of God. It is the source of all knowledge. The Qur'an, or the Book of Decree and Destiny as it could aptly be described, contains everything gross and subtle, the visible and the invisible laws, all of which interact.

The believers may be despondent about the fate of those who are not in Islam. Yet God says that this is the law, there is going to be *iman* (faith, trust, belief), and there is going to be *kufr* (denial, ingratitude). As we are created beings, it is useless and indeed impertinent to question the Creator. All that we can do is recognize the laws and submit to them, for we too are created according to these laws.

It is natural that those who have faith will wish the others to know the Qur'an and follow it. Yet some of creation are so gross that God says in a *hadith qudsi* (Divinely revealed tradition):

I have created them for the Fire and it does not matter (or affect me).

The foundation of the experiences in this world is based on duality, and this duality is Reàlity's method of teaching by discrimination and choice. In this world there is health and illness; man is programmed to desire health, so he will discover the laws that bring about health and those that cause illness. He will, therefore, choose to follow the first set and avoid the second. The Garden, which is the original abode, and the desired and sought after abode in this life, could only be experienced fully by the existence of its opposite — the affliction and turmoil of the fire.

God has created this world as a training ground and equipped us with the necessary means of interacting with and analyzing situations in order to understand their full meaning, see the unifying factor underlying them and thereby discover the structure behind all creation. The more we question the perfection of creation, the more we display our ignorance and isolation from Totality.

One of the key words in this *ayah* is *amr* which means command. The ultimate command belongs to God. Yet, we are part of that affair — a part that can reflect the meaning of the whole, and contains within it an understanding of the whole, and of the necessity of harmony with the whole.

Reality Guides to Itself, by Itself

> Whomsoever Allah guides, he is the one who follows the right way. And whomsoever He causes to err will be the losers.
>
> (7:178)

The above *ayah* shows the direct application to us of decree and destiny. Those people, who begin to really comprehend the meaning of the laws or the decrees that govern existence, and accept the bounds voluntarily, will know how to behave. They will not, for example, walk across the road just as a fast car is passing.

As for those who have learned the laws, yet abuse that knowledge and cross the road at the wrong time, they will be subjected to the 'hell' of the crash that will follow. Those who know and do not act are transgressing because consciously they are disconnecting their inner from the outer.

We have seen that, for those of us who are unaware of the laws, affliction is part of the education process through which we learn to avoid that which is not conducive to our state of well-being and eventually come to know those laws. Hence there is a positive element to it.

If, however, we have knowledge of these laws, yet still go against them, sheer hell (perfect justice) is let loose upon us, and we deserve the consequences. We cannot blame God or Nature for our sufferings. We are simply observing the outcome of cause and effect of the laws that govern our existence.

Heedlessness

> And certainly we have created for hell many of the jinn and the men. And they have hearts with which they do not understand, and they have eyes with which they do not see, and they have ears with which they do not hear; they are as cattle, nay, they are in worse errors; these are the heedless ones.
>
> (7:179)

The Qur'an says they have hearts but they do not have understanding, they have eyes but they do not see with them, and ears that they do not hear with; for the filter mechanism created by their desires and expectations ensures that they only see and hear what they want to see and hear.

The Excuses of the Prevaricators and the Role of the Prophets

> And they who claim association (with Allah) say: If Allah had pleased, we would not have served anything beside Allah, (neither) we nor our fathers, nor would we have prohibited anything without (an order from) Him. Thus did those before them; is then aught incumbent upon the apostles except a plain delivery (of the message).
>
> And certainly We raised in every nation an apostle saying: Serve Allah and shun the Shaytan. So there were some of them whom God guided and there were others upon whom error (loss) was due; therefore travel in the land, then see what was the end of the rejectors (deniers of truth).
>
> If you desire for their guidance, yet surely Allah does not guide him who leads astray, nor shall they have any helpers.
>
> (16:35–7)

When the Unity of the all-encompassing Reality is explained

16

to the spiritually unevolved being, his reaction is that if God wanted us to see everything as part of this Unity, He would have made us see that.

When the adamic consciousness was first created (made to rise) in the state of the heavenly garden, it was a consciousness of total harmony and equilibrium. The adamic nature is trusting and always desires the truth, for it was created to be in submission and obedience to truth. Adam had not heard falsehood until he listened to the voice of Shaytan. Man's inherent tendency is to seek the permanent, the reliable, the tranquil and avoid the distractions of Shaytan. Adam, however, not having heard anything other than the truth, was misled by Shaytan and only remembered the warning of God afterwards.

Thus arose the experience of duality — obedience and disobedience, truth and falsehood, tranquillity and agitation, gatheredness and dispersion. Adam had been created to evolve from a state of unquestioning obedience to one whereby his recognition and submission to the perfect will of his Creator would be founded on free will after duality and uncertainty had been experienced.

Man has been given the choice of recognizing the unific way, adhering to it and expanding within its bounds. Prophets are sent to confirm this state to man and to encourage him not to transgress the bounds, beyond which lies the abyss of destruction and loss, but instead to maintain himself by adoration and worship of the unific state, with full freedom of choice, in the safety of the haven (of being within the bounds).

This *ayah* is for those who are concerned that others be guided. Yet God will not guide those who are at a loss. A person is either guided or he is at a loss.

The Prophet as Transmitter of the Ways of Reality

> And We did not send any apostle but with the language
> of his people, so that he might explain to them clearly;
> then Allah makes whom He pleases err and He guides

17

whom He pleases, and He is the Mighty, the Wise.

(14:4)

The *ayah* explains how a Messenger connects with or relates to the people to whom he is sent, not only through language but also through the medium of their specific culture.

The *ayah* goes on to say that those who do not heed the message of God will be misguided or lost. God has made the laws, which are communicated by His Messengers, and it is incumbent upon us to learn these laws, if we wish to progress smoothly, happily and knowingly in this life.

The Gift of Discrimination

And Allah has created you and what you make.

(37:96)

God has given us the power to act, and He has given us '*aql* (faculty of reason, intelligence, discernment) that will guide our actions. This power of reasoning, which He has bestowed upon us, has in it the ability to check and correct our actions. So we are guided rather than misguided. The problem arises when we interfere with the faculties with which we are potentially endowed.

Why Diversity and Duality

And if Allah had pleased He would surely have made them a single community, but He makes whom He pleases enter into His mercy, and the unjust it is that shall have no guardian or helper.

(42:8)

God created man in diversity and a life on earth which is not in perfect harmony (outwardly) because it is the school in which mankind learns to apply his inner urge for equilibrium and contentment against an outer arena of action. The Creator could have imposed His will, as is the case with animals, had He wished to do so. The animals have no choice but to follow their physical impulses while man needs to learn and awaken to a code of conduct that will enable him to achieve his best innate tendencies. He has to learn the ways that will bring about desired states such as peace or good health.

The issue of being at a loss is parallel to doing oneself injustice. Man is programmed to dislike uncertainty and desire predictability and knowledge. No one likes unknowns. Therefore those who go against this innate tendency will cause themselves loss and the greatest injustice. God's love and mercy for His creation manifest themselves through the freedom He has given them, so when a person remains in the darkness of his limited animal self, he has only himself to blame; for these people there can be no guardian or helper, for they have overlooked the one and only all-encompassing, in-dwelling Guardian and Helper.

Why Some People Cause Themselves Injustice

> What! is he whose evil deed is made fairseeming to him so much so that he considers it good? Now surely Allah makes err whom He pleases and guides aright whom He pleases, so let not your soul waste away in grief for them; surely Allah is cognizant of what they do.
>
> (35:8)

If a person commits an evil action, he will invariably justify it and see his action as a positive one. The man is doing evil, but everyone wants to be in harmony; so perverted harmony is seeing a bad action as a good or appropriate one. His erroneous actions appear agreeable to him, because he has to live with himself. God has created us all with an awareness of *tawhid* (divine unity) within us, that enables us to personalize our situation, and make our own laws. There is only connectedness but there are degrees of it. This is why there is no possibility of a person progressing spiritually in separation. Man needs a community to interact with, otherwise he will fabricate his own laws.

19

The higher element in all of us makes us grieve for those who are at a loss. However, there is no point in emotionalism because we are powerless to change the laws of Reality. They must suffer from their mistakes, unless they choose the path of knowledge and action based upon the knowledge of those laws. God does not change people unless they change themselves.

The Disconnected Ones

> Surely We have placed chains on their necks, and these reach up to their chins, so they have their heads raised aloft.
>
> And We have made before them a barrier and a barrier behind them, then We have covered them over so that they do not see.
>
> And it is alike to them whether you warn them or warn them not: they do not believe.
>
> (36:8–10)

The people referred to in these *ayat* are disconnected. In front of them are barriers, behind them are barriers. They are not connected to the past for they do not see their present state as being the direct product of all the laws that were enacted upon them in the past — the good and the bad of it. They do not see the connection of the future as being a result of the way in which their will is unified with the Decree.

If their' will is the will of abandonment, they will see what has been decreed and there will be no barriers, for they will be unified with the Decree. However, people like those described above, whether they are warned or not, will never benefit from the light and knowledge of faith.

Ten Modes of *Qada'* as Revealed in the Holy Qur'an

The following are a collection of Qur'anic *ayat* on the different facets of *qada'* (destiny) as have been transmitted from the *Ahl al-Bayt*. All ten fundamental modes are associated as concomitants with the concept of destiny.

The first mode is that of *knowledge* as illustrated by

> ...And surely he was possessed of knowledge because We had given him knowledge, but most people do not know.
>
> (12:68)

This implies that the destiny of the Prophet Ya'qub (Jacob), to whom the *ayah* refers, was to come to know.

The second mode is *announcement*, that is to make something commonly known by 'announcing' it. God proclaims in:

> We had declared (make known) unto the Children of Israel in the Book:
>
> (17:4)

The third mode is that of *judgement*. The Arabic word for judge is '*qadi*'.

> Allah judges with the truth.... .
>
> (40:20)

The fourth mode is *saying*, which is shown in

> And We revealed to him this decree.... .
>
> (15:66)

The fifth mode has the meaning of *being done with something finishing, terminating*.

> But when We decreed death upon him.
>
> (34:14)

21

The idea expressed here is of something completed; for the affair is over when death is enforced.

The sixth mode is that of *order* or *command*.

> Your Lord has commanded that you shall not serve any but Him... .
>
> (17:23)

The seventh mode is that of *creation*.

> So He ordained them seven heavens in two periods, and revealed in every heaven its affairs; and We adorned the lower heaven with brilliant stars and (made it) to guard; that is the decree of the Mighty, the Knowing.
>
> (41:12)

Since God's creation takes place in biological time, there will be another sequence that will evolve in time, into which creation will move. Hence the seven heavens that lie layer upon layer, the least one of which is the physical heaven that we on earth witness and experience. This is the one referred to in the above *ayah*.

We are told that both heavens and earth were created in two periods or two modes. One possible meaning of this is that of the mode of the visible experiential state, and the mode of the inner forces and powers that are at play.

The eighth mode is that of *action*.

> Decide what you are going to decide (act).
>
> (20:72)

This means *exercise your judgement, act as you will, do what you want*. The emphasis being on *action* within the limitations of what you are able to decide; for your only freedom lies within this realm of action.

The ninth mode is that of *completion*.

> So when Musa had fulfilled the term, and he journeyed with his family.
>
> (28:29)

In this context it means to bring a matter to completion, to its end.

The tenth mode is the *close of an affair*. The concomitant here is in reference to *destiny with finality*.

> ...the matter is decreed concerning which you enquired.
>
> (12:41)

When it is said that affairs are all by the judgement of God, or by God's knowledge, it means that the matter is decreed concerning us who will experience it. God knows the situation according to the measure of what He is. God designates in the matter His judgement of what is right and what is not.

Summary

To summarize what we can glean from the *ayat* that have been quoted, '*qadar*' is the measure that apportions those laws of Reality, such as the laws of gravity, which are not going to change. It is absolute. The overall situation, if you take the environment, for example, may appear different — hot one day, windy the next — but the result is according to laws that are either superimposed or interactive with each other. These absolute forces or laws are understandable, discernible and sometimes measurable, but there is another projection to be considered: the interaction of the so-called 'self' with the external situation. The combination of these two factors results in you being either in harmony or disharmony.

If the extent of this tangent is a small one, one will say: 'What a tremendous day it is today.' It does not mean that there was anything more blessed in it than any other day, but the fact that one was in submission to whatever circumstances one found oneself in gave one the knowledge of how to interact with it; for without those two factors, decree (*qadar*) and the individual's action, nothing can happen.

Qada', judgement or destiny, is dependent upon the interaction between *qadar*, the decree, and the individual's state and action.

Imam 'Ali ibn Abi Talib said that the decree is like soul and action is like body. Soul without body cannot be discerned and body without soul has no life. The two combine to produce what is called destiny. This combination brings about a situation which is completely under the laws that govern existence, yet gives the individual a certain measure of freedom within these constraints, from which he may learn that the ultimate freedom is total abandonment into it, intelligently and experientially. This total abandonment is based on *yaqin* (certainty). The relative lack of resistence, which is the product of certainty, brings about a state of freedom.

Freedom should not be the superstitious abandonment to which some of us are prone. One can only say, 'If God wills,' for example, when one asserts one's existence, which is secondary, first. One may want, hypothetically, to build a house to give shelter to the people around. So one says, 'I want to build a house, if God wills.' This means that one has a wish, and in one's ignorance as to what events may transpire one is hopeful that one's wish and God's laws will coincide. This is why one says, 'If God wills', after expressing a certain view.

If one simply says, 'If God wills', it is a meaningless statement as everything is according to the will of God in the long term; even one's own will has been gifted to one so one can recognize its origin and its subservience to the Creator. The Source of all wills may be the same but the use to which each person puts it differs, as does the extent of its allotment to specific people through their lives.

Imagine the world as an Amusement Park, whose government has passed legislation to enable it to test the capabilities of its citizens. To do this they have created an entertainments park full of cars. The government has decreed the parameters of behaviour that are allowed in this park. There are many video cameras hidden to monitor the behaviour of the citizens. Most of them start by being very reckless in their handling of the cars. They bash up the vehicles until they learn the decree or system of the cars — ie, how long a distance it takes for the brakes to be effective, how long it takes to accelerate, and all the idiosyncrasies of the individual models. Once a player has fully comprehended the laws of this arena, he harmonizes and follows them, and his will and the ways of the cars coincide.

The government has no emotional concern as to whether some of the contestants in the Amusement Park have injured themselves through their experiments. The political and commercial machinery grind on, and the overall decree is not affected by the behaviour of any individual. They are easily replaceable; after all there are millions of them. The purpose of this experiment was to discover which of the contestants would emerge as a super unifier.

This is also the case with creation. The Creator of this world created according to the most precise laws. We are part of these overall laws but our own arena is a very limited one. If we can discern the laws that govern our inner and outer being, and unify our desires, intentions and actions with the overall decree, then we have succeeded. This state comes when we have stopped our expectations and desires. Then we have fully accepted our destiny because destiny is only our experience of the decree. Our only freedom lies in whether we choose to recognize this truth or not.

2

Affliction, the Ultimate Remedy

In considering the role of 'affliction' or 'testing' in man's spiritual development, we shall first examine the basic meaning in language of *fitnah* (affliction), which comes from the verb *fatana*, to try, tempt, seduce, afflict, torment. The dictionary definition of *fitnah* is *temptation, trial, charm, enchantment, captivation, fascination, enticement, intrigue, sedition, riot, discord, dissension.*

Like all enticements *fitnah* brings with it agitation and, therefore, torment. It implies in language a plot that is recognizable. The possibility of recognition gives us the opportunity to escape from its negative consequences. Love of one's children, for example, is an unavoidable affliction but the recognition of its universal occurrence is the doorway to its release. Indeed, that very recognition will bring about positive usefulness and advantage.

There are ten discernible modes associated with affliction and we will use the Qur'an to help analyze the concomitant modes.

One common mode of its meaning is *to be at a loss, to be confused*:

> They will cry out to them: Were we not with you? They shall say: Yea! but you caused yourselves to fall into temptation, and you waited and doubted, and vain desires deceived you till the threatened punishment of Allah came, while the arch-deceiver deceived you about Allah.
>
> (57:14)

The second meaning is *test*:

> ...and We tried you with (a severe) testing.
>
> (20:40)

> Do men reckon that they will be left alone on saying we
> believe and will not be tried (afflicted, tested)?
>
> (29:2)

> And most certainly We will try you until We have known
> those among you who exert themselves hard, and the pa
> tient, and made your case manifest.
>
> (47:31)

God's destiny is to unify so He wants His bondsmen to unify
what they say with what they are. This means man is constantly
being tested, as in a laboratory test, to gauge his mettle or true
state.

The third mode associated with its meaning is *proof* or *connection*

> Then their excuse would be nothing but that they would
> say: By Allah, our Lord, we were not idolaters.
>
> (6:23)

On the Day of Reckoning it will be clear to people that associating with other than God was the reason for their confusion and
loss; for idolatry is the outcome of association.

The fourth mode associated with the meaning of *fitnah* is *association* (*shirk*) — association in the sense of associating other beings with the transcendent Reality of God. In the following *ayah*
association is seen as the opposite of Divine unity (*tawhid*).

> And kill them wherever you find them, and drive them
> out from whence they drove you out, and persecution is
> worse (greater) than slaughter, and do not fight with them
> at the Sacred Mosque until they fight with you in it, but

if they do fight you, then slay them. Such is the recompense of the unbelievers.

(2:191)

The fifth mode is *denial, covering up*.

...Surely into trial (temptation) have they already fallen, and truly hell encompasses the disbelievers.

(9:49)

The sixth mode associated with its meaning is *persecution*.

Surely (as for) those who persecute the believing men and the believing women, then do not repent, they shall have the chastisement of hell, and they shall have the chastisement of burning.

(85:10)

The seventh mode is *agony, chastisement* or *distress*. This concept is reflected in the following three *ayat*.

Taste your persecution! this is what you would hasten on.

(51:13–14)

...and as for him whose temptation Allah desires, you cannot control anything for him with Allah.

(5:41)

The eighth mode is *death*, which is illustrated by the following two *ayat*:

...if you fear that those who disbelieve will cause you distress.

(4:101)

But none believed in Musa except the offspring of his people, on account of the fear of Pharaoh, and his chiefs, lest he should persecute them.

(10:83)

The ninth mode is *reflection*.

> And surely they had purposed to turn you away from that
> which We have revealed to you... .
>
> (17:73)

The tenth mode is *heavy distress*.

> Our Lord! do not make us a trial for those who disbelieve.
>
> (60:5)

> ...O our Lord! make us not subject to the persecution of
> the unjust people.
>
> (10:85)

In other words, do not cause us distress by those who are in
a state of infidelity. It is also said that the predominating meaning
of *fitnah* is love.

> And know that your wealth and your children are a temp-
> tation.
>
> (8:28)

This indicates that wealth and children are an affliction. Man
loves wealth and offspring so affliction and love are almost
equated. Anything other than love for God is a trial, unless one
loves them for God's sake. Then one passes the test, otherwise
one will suffer for the love here and now.

Once *fitnah* has set in and the disturbance has occurred, it can
be considered as *bala'*. This word has the meaning in language
of: *trial, tribulation, affliction, distress, misfortune, calamity. Bala'* is
from *ibtala*, which means *to test, afflict,* and *wear out* — *thiyabun
baliyah* are clothes that are threadbare. We are tested so that
which is not is worn off us. We are tried in order to recognize
that all the accoutrements of life are of little value. It is Reality's
way of making us wary of our desires.

Bala' is the bringing out to the light of experience that which
is written for us according to the measure. God, by His power,

29

has made afflictions the means by which our inner instincts will come forth and become visible, so that we can recognize the implications of punishment and reward. Our actions create an arena through which the knowledge of punishment and reward can be attained. We were created in order that we might reach our full potential; so affliction should not be seen as abstract chastisement. This is reflected in the following *ayah*:

> What! did you then think that We had created you in vain and that you shall not be returned to Us?
>
> (23:115)

Even the Prophets were subjected to terrible afflictions, as is shown by the following examples:

> And certainly we tried Sulayman, and We put on his throne a (mere) body, so he turned (to Allah).
>
> (38:34)

> He said: So surely we have tried your people after you, and the Samiri has led them astray.
>
> (20:85)

> And Musa chose out of his people seventy men for our appointment: so when the earthquake overtook them, he said: My Lord! if Thou hadst pleased, Thou hadst destroyed them before and myself (too); wilt Thou destroy us for what the fools among us have done? It is naught but Thy trial, Thou makest err with it whom Thou pleasest and guidest whom Thou pleasest... .
>
> (7:155)

Man's inherent tendency is to want only what is best because this is how the mercy and love of the Creator prevails. Hence our sufferings and difficulties should be viewed as assisting us along the path of spiritual progress by forcing us to give up all hindrances to our inner development.

The following *ayat* show how God uses *bala'* as a means by which He tests His bondsmen:

And We will most certainly try you with somewhat of fear
and hunger and loss of property and lives and fruits; and
give good news to the patient.

(2:155)

...but if they turn back, then know that Allah desires to
afflict them on account of some of their faults; and most
surely many of the people are transgressors.

(5:49)

...of you were some who desired this world and of you
were some who desired the hereafter; then He turned you
away from them that He might try you.

(3:152)

Surely We will try them as We tried the owners of the
garden... .

(68:17)

Who created death and life that He may try you — which
of you is best in deeds; and He is the Mighty, the Forgiving.

(67:2)

The interpretation of 'which of you is best in deeds' is which
of you has the highest inner intellect, power of discrimination
and proper action.

All *fitnah*, and therefore *bala'*, come about according to a system
of cause and effect. However, one can leave that system and be
saved from the *bala'*. At one level we are saved by the recognition
of how the *fitnah* and the *bala'* arose, and at a much more effective
level by severing from the cause of the difficulty.

An example of this is the *fitnah* of having a wife or a friend,
who is given to repeated periods of unreliablity and dishonesty.
The initial recognition, that one has fallen into a relationship
with a person who will continuously cause disruption to that
expected unity, brings about a certain healing or relief. The
knowledge of the irreconcilability of the situation itself must
bring relief, because love demands loyalty and reliablity, whereas
the erratic behaviour of the wife or friend cuts across all of these
factors.

This recognition is half the solution. Full relief can only be obtained after a final or total separation is brought about. So at first it was a *fitnah*, then the experience of *bala'*, then half relief, then full relief. This is an example of a *fitnah* and *bala'* from which one can evolve and learn.

In a society where a dictator comes to power and rules unjustly, it is a *bala'* that is brought about by the carelessness of the members of the community. God has created these systems of *fitnah* and *bala'* so that those beings who stray from the narrow path of correct conduct will experience trials and tribulations.

Many of these afflictions are to varying degrees remediable, as the preceding examples illustrate. However, if we stray too far off course, a point will come when we will be unable to obtain relief from the *bala'* and the decree becomes irreversible at least for a time; for example, a dictator whose power has become so firmly entrenched that only his death will release his people from their enslavement. Once a car has skidded and left the road there is no chance of stopping the workings of the laws of gravity. Equally, a man threatening to jump from a roof can be persuaded against his course of action, until the time he actually jumps.

There are some afflictions that are not reversible, and these will leave their effect on one's whole system. The loss of any faculty in the body, for instance, will close that door of information and knowledge forever. The death of a friend or family member, or the loss of men of knowledge to the community are irreparable losses. There may be compensating factors but compensation will not be specific.

There are other forms of afflictions, which are clearly man-made, and if these are allowed they will ultimately result in calamities, and indeed the collapse of a culture. It is important that we learn to differentiate between God's way and His mercy, and situations where man's greed or other lower elements can temporarily shield it. The Qur'an warns us of this:

> And among men is he who says: We believe in Allah; but
> when he is persecuted in (the way of) Allah he thinks the
> persecution of men to be as the chastisement of Allah;

and if there come assistance from your Lord, they would most certainly say: Surely we were with you. What! Is not Allah the best knower of what is in the breasts of mankind.

(29:10)

The question of commodity monopolies is a good example of this. If the price of a commodity is based totally upon its rarity or common availability, we can say that the expense or cheapness is directly attributable to the merciful Reality. We will then submit to the situation and be content with it. However, when this price is disturbed because of hoarding, dumping or other artificial means of control, it is clearly caused by man. There is a *hadith* in this respect:

He who brings forth what he needs will be well provided for and he who monopolizes is cursed.

If an individual or a group of people transgress and abuse the natural laws, their actions will affect many others adversely. Unless the others stop these erroneous actions or move out of their sphere of influence, they too will be influenced and affected by these injustices. These afflictions and injustices that beset innocent people are not a reflection of Divine will per se for the Divine Reality is just at all times. What we see here is limited injustice brought about by a person or a group, who were neither checked in time nor abandoned by the innocent ones. However, all of these human injustices are short-lived for cities, nations, and indeed total cultures will decay and collapse in the long run unless they abide by the immutable, unchangeable, just ways of God.

When we consider the different types of afflictions that may be suffered by seemingly innocent individuals or groups of people, we find that a child may have become blind or suffered from some incapacity due to the neglect or ignorance of his parents or guardian, while in other cases it is more difficult to relate the cause of suffering to human beings. Such events often cause people to suspect Divine injustice or imbalance.

This is not correct for the suspicion is based oñ incomplete information. Our judgement is only subjective and very limited. Unless we put the small picture in its totality we will only be judging an event in isolation. Even natural catastrophes are part of a greater network of cause and effect, which if viewed with a wider scope of understanding will be seen to be just. A handicapped child will cause his parents anxiety and hardship but a deeper understanding of the situation will reveal that constriction and trouble has sharpened the parent's sensitivity and awareness of subtler realities.

It is not possible to judge an event as being unjust when it is viewed over a short period of time. Many a door closes in one's face that, in the light of further experience and wisdom, will be seen as only the opening of new horizons. Equally acts of seeming injustice, when looked at from the wider time perspective, will fit into the overall picture.

At no time can we claim to have that overall vision which would enable us to relate all causes and their effects, for the systems and elements in existence are almost endless; their bounds connect with the world of unseen energies and subtler manifestations. Our insight and vision can only at best unravel a minute thread of the interrelatedness of cause and effect in this multi-dimensional web of existence. We are like small bats who can only chart and recognize a limited route in the endless cavern of the existential womb.

The role of affliction in man's spiritual growth is revealed in the following extract from a *hadith qudsi* (divinely revealed tradition):

> And there are amongst My believing bondsmen those whose belief will not be improved except by poverty and if I enrich them it will be ruined. And there are amongst My believing bondsmen those whose belief will not be improved except by enriching them and if I impoverish them it will spoil that. And there are amongst My believing bondsmen those whose belief will not be improved except by sickness and if I made their bodies healthy it would have

corrupted them. And there are amongst My believing bondsmen those whose belief will not improve except by good health and if I give them sickness it will cause them corruption. And I organize (manage the affairs) by My knowledge of what is in their heart for I am the All Knower.

The way that man is goaded and guided along his experiential life is according to what is most conducive to him in his real situation. He, in his ignorance, may see events as either being constrictive or expansive. Yet whatever form manifests will be the most appropriate for that individual's inner growth, and the believing person will know it is best for him.

3

Sayings of the Blessed Prophet and the Holy Imams

Introduction*

The aim of this book is to give a complete picture of the meaning of destiny and free will, without entering into philosophical debate or dwelling over much on academic niceties. Hence the direct usability and authenticity of the traditions is the key to this selection, and the book is restricted to a few references in order to keep its authenticity clear of doubts and divergences.

The majority of the traditions we will now examine are taken from the *Kitab al-Tawhid* (The Book of Unity) of Shaykh al-Saduq. Abu Ja'far Muhammad ibn 'Ali ibn Husayn ibn Musa ibn Babawayh al-Saduq al-Qummi, who is called the Chief of Hadith Narrators, was born in Qum in 306 AH/918 AD.

He is among the most revered authorities in Shi'a history and his studies are very well covered in traditional books. He is reported to have written more than three hundred volumes on the divine knowledges; two hundred and forty five of these volumes are recorded as having been copied but only a few of these have reached us in the present day. He is the author of one of the four source books of Shi'a Jurisprudence.

Shaykh al-Saduq's book on *tawhid*, from which the majority of the following Sayings are taken, is a collection of aspects of Unity, meanings of God's names and attributes and various discourses on spirituality. Commentaries on this book have been made by a number of great spiritual masters. It was printed in 1285 AH and there are also many known handwritten manuscripts.

The two other main sources of traditions, Shaykh al-Harrani and Fayd al-Kashani, were (respectively) the fourth century and tenth century after Hijrah authorities of their day.

Creation and the Command of God

The Blessed Prophet says:

> 'Truly Allah has created mankind and He knew in which direction they were heading. He bade them and forbade them. Whatever He ordered them to, He had made it possible for them to fulfill it. Whatever He had forbidden them from He had made it possible for them to abstain.'[1]

God's ways or the natural chains of cause and effect are in perfect harmony, bringing about natural justice and equilibrium. It is incumbent upon man to discover the means that will lead him to goodness and the bounds·that will protect him. As his intelligence develops, man will keep to the right path and will avoid the pitfalls. All this happens within God's creation for all creation has occurred with His knowledge and by His decree.

The Origin of Good and Evil

Imam Ja'far al-Sadiq has related the Blessed Prophet as saying:

> 'He who alleges that Allah, the Exalted, orders evil and indecency has lied upon Allah. And he who alleges that goodness and evil are beyond Allah's will has excluded Allah from His power. And he who alleges that disobediences are devoid of the power of Allah has lied upon Allah and he who has lied upon Allah, Allah will make him enter the Fire.'[2]

> We try you by evil and good by way of probation.
>
> (21:35)

We have a clear indication here that both 'good' and 'evil'

37

are subsumed under the all-encompassing power of God.

A companion of Imam Ja'far al-Sadiq said that he heard him saying:

> 'In the same way that the origin of goodness and provisions
> are from Allah, the Exalted, the origin of evil is from
> yourselves, even though the decree has permitted it.'[3]

It is related from Imam 'Ali ibn Abi Talib that one day he was questioned about the decree.

> He asked: 'Shall I speak briefly or at length?'
> His companions replied: 'But briefly.'
> He said: 'Allah is more splendid than to desire obscenity,
> and more glorious than to allow in His kingdom that
> which He does not intend.'[4]

Ultimately everything is according to God's decree but it is not God's decree that we perform evil actions. God's decree is that He wants us to discriminate, to recognize and follow what is good and avoid what is bad.

Compulsion and Delegation

The question was posed to Imam Ja'far al-Sadiq: 'Are humans compelled to their own actions?' The Imam replied:

> 'Allah, the Exalted, is more merciful upon His creation
> than to compel them to sins and to punish them for it.
> And Allah is more glorious than to want something that
> does not happen.'[5]

The nature of Reality is reflected in man's innate desire for goodness. We all desire good health and a peaceful life devoid of wants and upheavals. It is inconceivable that God, Who is the Source of all mercy and goodness, compels His creation to erroneous and sinful acts in order to punish them. Indeed punishment, which is feared, is created in order to deflect us from error.

God, the Glorious, has within His power all creational possibilities, so He is capable of all.

It is further related from Imam Ja'far al-Sadiq:

> 'People, as far as decree is concerned, are of three types. One man alleges that Allah forces people to sins. This man has wronged Allah in His judgement, and therefore he is a *kafir* [one who denies the truth]. Another alleges that the affair is delegated to them. He has weakened Allah's authority, thus he is a *kafir*. Thirdly a man alleges that Allah has ordered His bondsmen by virtue of what they are able to carry out, and that He does not expect of them what they cannot carry out. If he does well, he praises Allah; if he misbehaves he asks for forgiveness. This is the mature Muslim (who is capable of judgement).'[6]

The merciful Creator wants to show His creation His perfect justice and capability by creating them in such a manner that they actively participate in their spiritual evolution. So He only demands and expects from them what they are capable of. If they do well, they can only praise their Creator, and if they commit an error, they should recognize the nature of that error, see how it occurs, ask for forgiveness and return to the right path.

> It is related that Muhammad ibn 'Ajlan said:
> I asked Imam Ja'far al-Sadiq:
> 'Has Allah delegated the affairs to his bondsmen?'
> The answer was:
> 'Allah is more generous than to delegate to them. Allah is far too just to compel a bondsman to action and then to chastise him for it.'[7]

The subject matter dealt with in this *hadith* is similar to that discussed in the preceding traditions in this section, so the same commentaries apply.

On this same point the following saying is related from Imam 'Ali al-Rida. Mention was made of 'compulsion' and 'delegation', and the Imam said:

> 'Shall I not give you a foundation on this issue so that you will never differ over it anymore nor quarrel with anyone but that you overcome him?'
> And he said:
> 'Allah, the Exalted, is not obeyed by compulsion nor is He disobeyed by being overcome, nor does He ignore His bondsmen in His kingdom. He is the owner of what He has made them own and capable upon what He has made them capable of.'[8]

The nature of creation is such that we are not separate from its totality. So that man may be shown that total interconnection the Creator has given him his innate tendencies and his faculty of reasoning. This enables man to follow the natural laws by his own choice. When he does this, obedience to God's will becomes his chosen path, rather than forced submission.

God's mercy is such that there is a limit to the extent man is able to transgress and wreak havoc. Indeed all man's capabilities are within and subservient to God's capabilities. His nature encourages him to unify with the intended laws. When he chooses to transgress, he is going against his nature and God's will. This life affords him all the possibilities to discover this fact for himself.

The following *hadith* is quoted from Imam Ja'far al-Sadiq:

> 'It is neither compulsion nor delegation. It is a matter between two affairs.'
> And the Imam was asked:
> 'What is a matter between two affairs?'
> He replied:
> 'The parable of that is like a man whom you saw about to commit a sin and you forbade him against it but he did not listen, so you left him and he commited that sin. The fact that he did not accept your order and your leaving him does not make you the one who ordered him to sin.'[9]

God's way is to discourage man from committing errors and sins or doing anything that brings about a state of disequilibrium. However, if man chooses to transgress, it is not God Who has ordered him to do this. It is man's erroneous choice. The suffering that comes from his error is created to deflect him back to the correct path. It is an act of love and mercy, not of punishment.

> Imam 'Ali al-Rida was asked:
> 'Has Allah delegated His affair to His bondsmen?'
> The Imam said:
> 'Allah is more dignified than that.'
> The man said:
> 'So has He compelled them to sins?'
> The Imam said:
> 'Allah is more just and wise than that.'
> Then the Imam said:
> 'Allah, the Exalted, has said: "O Son of Adam, I am more worthy of good deeds than you. You are more worthy of yours sins than I. You have committed sins with the power that I placed in you." '[10]

It may be inferred from this *hadith* that the power God has bestowed upon man has been given to him so that, through his experimentation with this power, he may be enabled to grow in excellence and move along the path of God's decree in peace, tranquillity and knowledgeable submission.

In the following *hadith* Imam Ja'far al-Sadiq is asked:

> 'Inform me regarding the differences that occur amongst our followers.'
> The man added:
> 'It is with regard to compulsion and delegation.'
> The Imam said:
> 'Then ask me.'
> The man said:
> 'Has Allah compelled His bondsmen to commit sins?'
> The Imam said:
> 'Allah is a greater compeller than that.'

The man then asked:
'Has He delegated it to them?'
The Imam said:
'Allah is more capable (powerful) upon them than that.'
The man said:
'What is then this affair? May Allah give you the best of states.'
The Imam turned his hand up and down two or three times, then said:
'If I answered you, then I would commit *kufr*.'[11]

There is an apparent conflict that exists between 'compulsion' and what appears to be the freedom bestowed upon man.

The Imam, knowing that God is the all powerful Creator of all, cannot intimate that man has any power over others than that which comes from God. Although it appears to man that he has a certain power by delegation, the assumption that this power has been bestowed upon him would be regarded as an aspect of *shirk*. God is One. All affairs are from Him, by Him, to Him. It is for this reason that the Imam wishes to resolve an apparent conflict without adding further to the confusion by covering up the truth.

Once man looks deeply into the certain measure of freedom that he has, he discovers that in order for him to attain an optimum state, there is only one specific choice for each situation that confronts him — although he may not realize at the time what this choice is.

The Creator has created according to specific laws that do not change. What changes is the orientation of those who apply these laws and their specific application.

This question is difficult to expound upon and requires much subjective reflection. The more one expounds upon it outwardly, the deeper the subject becomes and the greater the likelihood of the confusion that invariably arises when the effulgent truth is concealed and ignorance ensues.

It is related that a man came to Imam 'Ali ibn Abi Talib.

'O Commander of the Faithful, inform me about the decree.'
The Imam replied:
'It is a deep sea. Do not enter into it.'
The man asked:
'O Commander of the Faithful, tell me about the decree.'
The Imam said:
'It is a dark road, do not set foot on it.'
The man then said:
'O Commander of the Faithful, inform me about the decree.'
The Imam said:
'It is Allah's secret, so do not carry that burden.'
The man said again:
'Inform me about the decree.'
The Imam said:
'If you refuse my advice, I will ask you: Was the mercy of Allah before the deeds of the bondsmen or were the deeds of the bondsmen before the mercy of Allah?'
So the man said in reply:
'The mercy of Allah was bestowed upon the bondsmen before their deeds.'
The Imam said:
'Get up and greet your brother, for now he has embraced Islam and before that he was a *kafir*.'
And the man went away, but not far. Then again, the man turned to Imam 'Ali and asked him:
'Is it by the original wish of Allah that we get up, sit, and are constricted and expanded?'
So the Imam commented:
'You are still within the (original) wish (of Allah), but I would ask you three things. Tell me, did Allah shape His bondsmen as He wished or as they wished?'
The man said:
'As He wished.'
The Imam said:
'Did Allah create bondsmen for what He wants them or for what they want?'
The man answered:
'For what He wants.'

43

The Imam said:
'Do they come to Him on the Day of Judgement as He wants them or as they want?'
The man said:
'They will come to Him as He wants them.'
The Imam said:
'Now get up. There is nothing more for you as far as the will of Allah is concerned.'[12]

So far we have seen from the preceding traditions that there is no delegation, yet individuals do have responsibility. This is what is meant by free will. It is to be understood that this will is encompassed within God's will. So ultimately it is God's will that prevails.

When Imam 'Ali ibn Abi Talib asked of the man: 'Was the mercy of God before the deeds of the bondsmen?' and the man replied: 'Yes', his affirmation signified that man's inherent tendency is to adore and worship God; for this is the purpose of His creation.

When Imam 'Ali further asked the man to inform him of three things concerning the will of God, the man confirmed that God creates the bondsmen as He wills, that God creates the bondsmen for what He wants, and that the bondsmen will come to Him on the Day of Reckoning as He wants them. By this it is meant that although our behaviour and actions may be manifested in diverse and seemingly contradictory ways, all of our actions stem from one Source, the Divine Reality, from Whom all comes.

Imam Ja'far al-Sadiq is quoted as saying:

'Neither compulsion nor delegation but a station between the two stations.'[13]

The Imam describes this "station between two stations" as follows:

"Goodness of character, emptiness of the chest (purification of the innermost), respite in time, provision for the

44

journey, and the causes that make a person embark on an action."[13]

This saying describes the entire journey of man in this life. First he must develop his character, which also includes his faculties, discrimination and the growth of his *'aql* if he is to reach a high level of cognizance. Man is the highest among creation for he is the only creature that has a rational self that can express itself. It is about man that God has revealed:

> ...thus has He made them subservient to you, that you may magnify Allah because He has guided you aright; and give good news to those who do good (to others).
>
> (22:37)

> And He it is Who has made the sea subservient that you may eat fresh flesh from it and bring forth from it ornaments which you wear.
>
> (16:14)

There are many *ayat* in the Qur'an that show man has been given the potential to reach the highest state:

> Certainly We created man in the best of forms.
>
> (95:4)

> Allah does not impose upon any soul a duty but to the extent of its ability; for it is (the benefit of) what it has earned, and upon it (the evil of) what it has wrought.
>
> (2:286)

So within the capacity that has been bestowed upon the individual, each can attain the fullness of his character. Also no faculty is taken away unless a replacement is given. The weakening of eyesight with age, for example, can be compensated by the growth of insight and wisdom. It is up to the individual as he grows older to gain the inner knowledge that will make up for his naturally deteriorating physical sight.

Regarding the second aspect in this tradition, which is the 'emptiness of the chest', man must try to purify himself and render his heart clear and pure.

The third station is a 'respite in time', so that man is given the opportunity to experiment and learn what is right for him — ie, what is dictated by his primal state and what is not.

The fourth station is 'provision for the journey' so that he gains the right provisions and recognizes that the real poverty is poverty of knowledge.

The final station, 'the causes that make a person embark on an action', is for the individual to discover that every action is the result of an intention. These intentions emanate from the innermost; the purer the intention, the clearer and more effective the action. We see from this the importance of the connection between actions and intentions. If this does not exist, hypocrisy will prevail.

> ...They say with their mouths what is not in their hearts;
> and Allah best knows what they conceal.
>
> (3:167)

There is an admonishment for those who are weak in the faith in:

> O you who believe! why do you say that which you do
> not do?
>
> (61:2)

On the other hand, there may be situations where a person has to say something he does not believe in because he is under pressure. In this case the person may be reprieved:

> ...not he who is compelled while his heart is at rest on
> account of faith.
>
> (16:106)

> Allah does not call you to account for what is vain in your
> oaths, but He will call you to account for what your hearts

46

have earned, and Allah is Forgiving, Forbearing.

(2:225)

In other words, God will not hold you responsible for what is not really meant.

If a person studies the meaning of these five characteristics he will reach the conclusion that man's destiny is determined to some degree by creational limitations, but he also possesses a certain measure of freedom, which is delineated by set bounds.

It is related that Imam 'Ali al-Rida said:

> 'Shall I not give you in this respect a foundation that you will not differ over nor can anyone argue with you regarding it, but that you overcome his argument?'
> They said:
> 'If you think it proper.'
> The Imam said:
> 'Allah, be He exalted, is not obeyed by sheer force nor is He disobeyed by being overcome and He does not neglect His bondsmen in His kingdom. For He is the owner of what He has made them capable of. If His bondsmen acknowledge and adhere to His obedience, He does not cause that not to emanate nor will He cause it to be deprived or not to take place. And if they disobey and He wishes to be between them and that action, He will certainly do so. And if He does not intervene and they have carried out that action, it is not He who has put them into it. And he who understands the full bounds of this speech will overcome whoever argues with him.'[14]

God wants man, His highest creation, to appreciate the primal laws of creation, to see that they are in perfect harmony, majesty and beauty, and to recognize that these laws are for his benefit. The laws span a very wide spectrum which encompasses all physical laws and physical realities as well as the subtler non-physical laws functioning in time and space; most of which are beyond the grasp of the mind and intellect. They are also the laws that link physical realities with the non-physical non-spatial

47

Truth. They include the sub-atomic world with its subtle inter-changes between matter and energy. Man is not separate from these laws, nor is he independent of the Lawmaker. He must test and experience the laws until he learns to submit to them and thereby be saved. This is the true meaning of surrender.

The Creator will never be overcome, nor will His creation be damaged or halted by man's transgressions. The Creator has not neglected His creation in His kingdom for they are all subject to certain limits and bounds. However, within these limitations they are given the freedom to exercise their faculty of reasoning, and to learn that obedience and submission is the only way for efficient, successful survival and subsequent awakening. The intelligent man soon realizes that he has no power of his own. His power is loaned to him for the duration of his life on this earth. If he chooses to act correctly then it can be regarded as his choice. The knowledge of that choice is an inner awareness or conscience that man has been endowed with. However, if a man makes a mistake, the blame is not God's. It is he, himself, who has put himself in that position by his ignorance, or his misplaced desires or expectations.

This *hadith* gives us the whole of the meaning of freedom and constraints. We are free to know what is right and wrong. We are free to enjoin the right and stop at the bounds of the wrong. We are free to make certain changes in our environment inwardly and outwardly within set limits. We have neither the freedom of absolute power nor of infinite life. We are free to taste the state of inner freedom and timelessness through total abandonment.

This world is like a child's playpen, which has been created in order for us to have a testing ground, whereby to the extent of our ability we are given the opportunity to recognize the truth behind creation, and to acknowledge that the purpose behind our creation is the recognition of the glorious Creator, Whose nature is beyond limitations and time, and Who permeates and absorbs all His creations, thereby unifying them in a total network. The knowledge of this truth is the ultimate awareness which creation seeks in all its endeavours.

When a person awakes to this realization, he has saved himself. If he does not, he will be afflicted because he is transgressing his Creator's laws. These afflictions can have a positive outcome and become the cause of his awakening, by forcing him to acknowledge his limitations, and seek guidance, knowledge and re-direction.

An Injunction of Jurisprudence

Imam 'Ali al-Rida was heard to say on the position between compulsion and delegation:

> 'He who says it is compulsion, do not give him of *zakat* (poor tax) nor accept his witnessing. Allah does not expect from anyone except his maximum capability, nor does Allah place upon anyone more than he is able to bear. No self will earn except what is due to it. And no soul shall be burdened with another soul's burden.'[15]

If, after exposure to the Holy Qur'an, the Prophetic explanation and the elaborations of the Imams on the personal responsibility and relative freedom of man, a person still insists that God compels him to wrong actions, all we can do is isolate him from the community. We should not give him alms nor accept him as a witness. God has not made us responsible for the wrongdoings of others.

Will and Power

It is related from Imam 'Ali ibn Abi Talib that the Prophet said:

> 'Allah, be He exalted, says: O Son of Adam, it is by My will that you can will for yourself; and by My wish that you can wish; and by the grace of My blessings upon you that you had the strength to be disobedient; and by My protection, aid and goodness to you that you have been able to perform your obligations to Me. Thus I am more

worthy of your good deeds than you, and you are more worthy of your evil deeds and wrong doings than Me. Goodness is from Me for you by My beginning and delegating it to you. And evilness is from Me to you according to what you have reaped as a punishment. And it is by My kindness to you that you have the power to obey (Me, and) it is because of your misjudgement of Me that you have become despondent of My mercy. So praise is for Me and proof is upon you by clear evidence and I will have My way upon you because of disobedience.

'The reward of your good deeds rests with Me by good action. I have not neglected warning you nor have I deprived you whenever you have embarked on action, nor have I expected from you more than your capabilities, nor have I burdened you with trusts except to your ability to bear them and take upon yourself also. I am content in Myself with you in accordance with your contentment in yourself with Me. I have accepted from you to Myself what you have accepted to yourself from Me.'[16]

It is related from Imam Ja'far al-Sadiq:

'Allah has ordered and did not wish, and had the wish but did not order. He gave Iblis [Satan] the order to prostrate but He did not want him to prostrate himself for if He wanted he would have prostrated himself. And He forbade Adam from the eating of the tree, yet His wish was that Adam could eat from it because if He did not wish Adam could not have eaten.'[17]

It is related from Imam 'Ali ibn Abi Talib:

'Allah has two types of wills and wishes [desires]: the will of certainty and the will of intention. He prohibits but He wishes it. He orders but He does not wish it. Do you not see that He ordered Adam and his wife 'Do not eat from the tree' but He wished it (to be). And if He did not wish them to eat from that tree, the will of their desire would not have overcome Allah's desire.'[18]

God gave Adam the power to choose. He warned Adam, who was in the Garden where all his needs were fulfilled, against the Tree (desire), but Adam would not have known the disgrace or disadvantage of that action until he had done it. So Adam's will to disobey existed only because God had permitted him the possibility of disobedience. Adam had only been obedient up to that point. He also obeyed Shaytan (through forgetfulness because he had been pre-warned against Shaytan). So it was Adam, not God, who was responsible for this act of disobedience.

The overall purpose of creation is for man to waken to the knowledge of his Creator, by recognizing the ways of the Creator and the actions of the Creator within him and without. Man cannot under any circumstance overcome God's total acceptable wish. It is within God's wish that man will transgress in order that he might discover the meaning of transgression and remember that God has created him with the capacity of suffering the consequences of transgression.

Man is the ultimate creation because he contains within himself a basic awareness, which tells him what is right and what is wrong. As there is also an experiential Reality that confirms this, he is set on an autonomic system of self-correction, unlike the animals, who do not have this knowledge and are hence constricted.

The Extent of the Capability of the Bondsman

It is related that 'Abayah ibn Ruba'i al-Asadi asked Imam 'Ali ibn Abi Talib about *istita'ah* (ability, capability).

The Imam said:
'You asked about your ability, that you may possess it with God or beside God?'

'Abayah kept quiet

The Imam again asked:
'Tell me, O 'Abayah?'

And he said:
'But what shall I say?'

The Imam said:
'If you say that you possess it with Allah I will kill you, and if you say that you possess it beside Allah I will kill you.'

So 'Abayah said:
'O Commander of the Faithful, then what shall I say?'

The Imam said:
'You ought to say that you possess it by Allah, Who possesses it irrespective of you and if He bestows it upon you it is His gift, and if He slips it off you that is His affliction. For He is the owner of what He has enabled you to own and He is capable of what He has enabled you to be capable of. Have you not heard people asking about "*la hawlah wa la quwwata illa bi'llah*" [there is no power nor capability except by Allah]?'

'Abayah then said:
'What does it mean?'

The Imam said:
'(There is) no way of diverting from disobedience to Allah except by taking refuge in Allah (except by the protection of Allah) and there is no power for us to obey Allah except by the help of Allah.'

'Abayah then jumped up and kissed his hands and feet.[19]

If God strips us of our power or capability in any way, it is an affliction from Him, in order that we may be tested. God's relationship with His bondsmen, in this respect, can be compared with that of a father with his son. The father has already taught the boy about good and evil, about the limitations that exist in this life, and the responsibilities that are upon him. He has also informed the son that his present dwelling is not permanent, and the nature of his permanent abode will be determined by the extent of his good and evil actions.

The father is so patient and compassionate with his son that he gives him the freedom to make some mistakes. He tells him that if he follows the prescribed path he will eventually reach the Garden, where there is nothing other than goodness and equilibrium. However, if he chooses to stray, he will earn for

himself through his wrongdoing an inferior situation. This freedom of action that is given to the son is the same as the capability
that has been bestowed upon all the sons of Adam, and the
examples we have been given to guide us to a correct way of life
are the lives of the Prophets and those who followed them.

The Interrelationship Between Decree, Action and Destiny

Imam Ja'far al-Sadiq said:

> 'Decree and destiny are two creations (or attributes) from
> Allah's creation. Allah increases in His creation what he
> wishes.'[20]

This *hadith* means that there are two creations in the sense of
two systems, each with its own intricate laws. Before creation,
neither measures nor destinies existed. Decree and destiny are
stages into which creations are caught, evolved and changed,
until eventually they reach their final visible destinies in God,
Who can increase or reduce in His creation what He wills.

It is related that someone said to Imam 'Ali Zayn al-'Abidin:

> 'May Allah make me be sacrificed for you. Is it by decree
> that people will receive that which comes to them or by
> their actions?'
> The Imam said:
> 'Decree and action are to one another like soul and body;
> for the soul without a body cannot sense, and the body
> without a soul is a picture with no motion in it. And if
> they combine they will gain strength and usefulness. This
> is how action and decree are. For if decree had fallen upon
> action, you would not have known the Creator from the
> created. And decree would be something that you would
> not have sensed. And if action was not in line with the
> decree, it would not pass to completion, but by their union
> they gain strength and in Allah there is aid for His right-
> eous bondsmen.'[21]

Decree has been attributed to God in the sense that He has moulded it and set its bounds, its being and non-being.

> Surely We have created everything as a measure (decree).
>
> (55:49)

If it were not according to a measure, the outcome of the laws would not have been known. And the action of the man interacts with what is for him, and what is incumbent upon him.

Therefore, the decree of God, as far as it concerns man's covenant with God, will not be complete upon a being except by his actions. He has to act in order that the decree be felt. Action and decree are like body and spirit; without a body nothing is felt, without actions the decree will not be understood. However, decree is the origin of the place of enactment. Action is from where decree descends or is manifested.

Imam 'Ali Zayn al-'Abidin continued:

> 'The most tyrannical of all beings is he who sees his tyranny as justice and the justice of the guided ones as tyranny. Is it not the case that the bondsman has four eyes: two eyes through which he sees the affairs of his next life, and two eyes through which he sees the affairs of this world? If Allah wants good for a bondsman, He will open his two eyes which are in his heart, so that He observes with them his faults;'[21]

(Another reference to this saying gives the following as the last phrase: 'He sees by them the unseen'). If we see our faults and isolate them, the rest which we have not seen will become clearer.

The Saying continued:

> 'And if He wills other than that, He will leave the heart with what is in it.'
> Then the Imam turned to the man, who had asked him about the decree and told him:
> 'This is from Him and that is from Him.'[21]

54

By this the Imam means that the opening of the 'eyes of the heart' or the leaving of them is of the decree. This signals that the knowledge of the secret of the decree and contentment by it is for him whose heart's eye has opened.

Here is an indicator of one of the secrets. The knowledge of the secret of the decree lies in contentment; for it is contentment that opens the inner eye.

One cannot have two things in the heart at the same time. If love of this world is in the heart, the love of the other world is out of it. So how can the heart's eye for the next world open if it only contains this world? The Imam is hinting about contentment. It is this contentment that enables one to understand the secret of the decree.

If we want to know the decree, we must cease knowing anything else. We must not be concerned or interested in knowing this or that situation. Then we will know the ultimate situation which this or that situation either stems from or is a part of. This is an admixture of pure power and the individual will, the latter resulting from the degree of ignorance or knowledge possessed by the various individuals concerned.

God's Covenant with Man

A man said to Imam Ja'far al-Sadiq:

> 'May I be sacrificed for you. What do you say concerning decree and destiny?'
> He replied:
> 'I say that Allah, the Exalted, when He collects His bondsmen on the Day of Reckoning, will ask them about His covenant with them and He will not ask about His destiny upon them.'[22]

God's covenant is ingrained in the heart of His creation. Man is, at all times, seeking his inner and outer harmony. He desires unification and dislikes dispersion; knowledge and love are sought because they unite and cement.

The worlds of matter and physical senses are only a laboratory for us to discover that we are already united and controlled by our Creator. Waking up and acknowledging this Reality is upholding the covenant.

The actual existential environment in which we are placed is our destiny. Although there is a relationship between the degree of the individual's destiny and the relevant environmental factors, we know that a serious seeker will reach for and surrender to his covenant, irrespective of what is around him. In fact, the greatest upholders of God's covenant, the Prophets, were destined to live under circumstances that would seem more likely to have hindered rather than enhanced their quest for realisation, for many suffered a great deal of restriction and constriction regarding the physical world.

God will neither question us nor make allowances for the outer set-up in which we have been placed, rather we will be questioned about the degree of our realisation of the purpose of His creation. We will be asked about whether we have utilized our position and circumstances to the utmost and the extent of our adherence to its laws — ie, the covenant between God and His creation.

One's individual destiny and the particular role one finds oneself playing is like a script in the theatre of life. In this parable of destiny, the covenant is our responsibility to know the Scriptwriter, and the reason behind the play. We are programmed sufficiently towards that end by the driving powers within ourselves. If those driving powers are guided by growing discrimination then our lusts and desires will end up in modesty and contentment; our angers and expectations will turn to courage and patience. This will result in total surrender to the will of the Scriptwriter, with its ensuing exposure to Divine knowledge, thereby fulfilling the covenant.

The details of the script and the specific role of the actor, therefore, are of little relevance when one is questioned by the Scriptwriter. They are only relevant to the actor himself, who is so absorbed in his role that he is blind to everything else. God's mercy is manifested in the continuously changing roles He presents to His actors but, if the poor actor fails to realize the object

of the exercise, which is submission and acceptance of the script
as it reaches him, his blindness will imprison him within his own
role, and those limitations will be his hell.

Specific individual destinies are of small significance in regard
to the discovery of the Limitless; for the Owner of the entire
world there is little difference between he who owns ten dollars
and he who has ten million.

Knowledge of the Decree

Whilst Imam 'Ali ibn Abi Talib was marshalling his troops
on the day of the Battle of Siffin, Mu'awiyah was awaiting
him impatiently. Imam 'Ali was upon a horse of the Blessed Prophet, in his hand was the spear of the Blessed
Prophet, and he was wearing the two pronged sword. One
of his companions said to the Imam:
'Be on your guard, O Commander of the Faithful, for I
fear that this cursed one will assassinate you.'
The Imam said:
'If you are saying that he is not to be trusted with respect
to his religion and he is the most accursed of those who
came out against the guided ones, it is right. But it is
sufficient for me that I have destiny as my guard.

'There is no one unless he has with him angels that
protect him from falling into wells, or when a wall falls
on him, or from any other evil that may afflict him. And
when his destined time comes to him, these angels leave
him to what is coming to him and what is going to afflict
him.

'And as for me, when the appointed time comes, the
most evil of them will come forth and will sever this from
that (pointing to his beard and head) and will move this
from that. It is a firm appointment, and it is a promise
that has no lie in it.'[23]

If we consider the example of the child playing in the playground, we can infer that initially the child has been given a small
module to experiment with. If he behaves according to the laws,
then he will be exposed to more, for he has shown that he can

be trusted. This is what is meant by certainty in the spiritual sense.

Certainty comes to us if we have been able to take the responsibility for the knowledge of destiny. Otherwise, it is barred from us because we are still preoccupied with our own small affairs. The certainty that comes to the hearts of the Prophets, Imams, the *awliya'* (friends of God) or the righteous people resembles a window opening onto a scene, which we are only permitted to glimpse if we are not going to be shocked or frightened by what we see. This will only happen when nothing of the self remains.

Insights into the future are only given to those who can take the burden. How else could these people have exposure to certain knowledge of future events, yet still function and behave completely as though nothing had touched them?

This is why Imam 'Ali ibn Abi Talib has said: 'It is a dark road, do not be on it.' Imam 'Ali had been informed by the Blessed Prophet in detail throughout his life *how* he was going to die and when. Yet, if the majority of us knew we were going to suffer an injury tomorrow, it would block most of our energy from now until then in anticipation of the event.

A heart must be disconnected from anything else for its inner eye to open up upon true destiny. The key to this knowledgeable abandonment and the test of it is contentment with the decree. When these conditions are fulfilled, one unifies with the decree.

> One day, 'Imam 'Ali ibn Abi Talib moved away from a leaning wall to another wall. People asked him:
> 'Do you run away from destiny?'
> Whereupon he answered:
> 'I have run from Allah's destiny to Allah's decree.'[24]
> [When he got up, the wall fell.]

Destiny is the end product of decree. Destiny is the judgement. It is the seal of the decree. We have reached the end when we have reached our destiny. So when Imam 'Ali said that he was running from destiny to the decree of God, he meant that God had decreed that he should avoid the leaning wall through giving him the faculty of reason and sight. He was moving along what

God had decreed, for the decree on this occasion was for him to move.

> It was said to the Commander of the Faithful
> 'Shall we not guard you?'
> Imam 'Ali replied:
> 'Every man's destiny is his guardian.'[25]

Let us compare the two traditions. In one case, Imam 'Ali moved along towards what was decreed; in the other he was shown that it was decreed for him to remain where he was. It is a question of the degree of *yaqin* (certainty). *'Ilm al-yaqin* (knowledge of certainty) relates to theoretical knowledge such as the knowledge of pain, when one has an accident. *'Ayn al-yaqin* (eye of certainty) is the experiential aspect of this knowledge, the experiencing of pain, the witnessing of the Fire, the knowledge that the decree will occur. *Haqq al-yaqin* (truth of certainty) is the absolute truth of pain, of actually being in the Fire or being fully in total harmony with one's destiny.

The station of the Imam was that of *haqq al-yaqin* for being the manifestation of an unfolding destiny he simply enacted the decree. He was the voice of destiny, whereas a spiritually attuned person is attempting to acquire *'ilm al-yaqin*.

If one has managed to exclude everything else from the heart and is moving along by the 'two eyes of the heart' as described by Imam 'Ali Zayn al-'Abidin, then one is running along the path of one's decree; for there is no longer any resistance. If, however, one is not in a state of continuous contentment, the discordant self within will continue to fan the flames of agitation and disharmony.

It was said to Imam 'Ali ibn Abi Talib when he wanted to fight with those who came out against him:

> 'Would not it be better if you take care and be on your guard?'
> Imam 'Ali declared:
> 'Which day should I run away from death? Is it the day

which was not destined or is it the day of destiny? On the day that has not been destined I have no fear of anything else. And if it has been destined for me no amount of caution will be of good to me.'[26]

It is related that once Imam Husayn ibn 'Ali met with Mu'awiyah. Mu'awiyah asked him:

'What has come upon your father that he fights the people of Basra?'

Mu'awiyah is referring to the Battle of Jamal when Sayyida 'A'isha went against Imam 'Ali ibn Abi Talib.

Imam Husayn ibn 'Ali said:
'What made him do that is his knowledge that what will reach him will never miss him and what will miss him will never reach him.'[27]

Man lives in time. He experiences destiny, which follows the decree and interacts with it, in time. During this process he sometimes thinks that the power and result emanate from him, until finally he concludes that, in reality, he is only a witness to the Divine creation, and the Divine decree is for him to recognize the one Creator, by whose grace he was brought about so that he might witness His perfect way. True witnessing of this perfection can only occur when the individual reaches a state of total submission and non-duality. When this state is perfected the individual personality melts with the total flow of events. The higher consciousness of what remains of him may then be exposed to future events.

The more the personality of the individual is assertive, the more the separation from Reality; the lower the spiritual state of the being, the more merciful it is that he does not know his destiny. However, for the person of total abandonment, who transcends the cage of time, present and future become one. God, then, allows these visions.

When Imam Husayn ibn 'Ali was leaving Mecca on the Day of Hajj 61 AH, rational advice was given to him that he was going to confront a great evil force. The Imam's reply to this counsel was: "God has wished to see me martyred." The Imam had the privilege of seeing his physical destiny, for his spirit and consciousness was at such a level that he could witness what would happen to his body with complete contentment and submission.

When people contemplate the greatness of his sacrifice, they are measuring it from their individual, egotistic, dual consciousness; for the Imam, himself, there could be no sacrifice, because sacrifice entails someone who is sacrificing and a thing to be sacrificed. For him who sees only God and exists in that unific state, there is no giver, no taker, only the one Reality that transcends all of these; for such a being leaving this world is real liberation for he knows that death belongs only to the body and that his real self will move on to the next phase of eternal consciousness.

The Nature of Action

The following saying is related from Imam Husayn ibn 'Ali.

> The Imam said:
> 'I heard my father, Imam 'Ali say: "Actions are according to three states — obligatory ones, virtuous ones, and disobediences. As for the obligatory ones, they are by the order of Allah, glory be to Him, by the contentment of Allah, by the destiny that Allah has decreed, and by the decree of Allah and His measures, and His will and by His knowledge.
>
> "As for the virtuous deeds, they are not by the order of Allah but they are by His contentment according to the judgement of Allah and the measure of Allah, and His will and by His knowledge.
>
> "As for the disobedient acts, they are not by the order of Allah. But they are according to the judgement of Allah

61

and measure (decree) of Allah and His will and knowledge.
And He punishes according to it." '28

Look at the fine distinction between the states. They all fall
under the same category for they are by decree and by destiny,
by will and by knowledge. The only difference is that there are
those actions which are absolute, emanating by the order of God,
and there are those which are either virtuous or disobedient,
and will be rewarded or punished accordingly.

Shaykh al-Saduq, who collected most of the traditions referred
to in this book, quoting from another saying says:

> 'Nothing happens in the heavens or earth unless there are
> seven elements in it — desire (*mashwah*), will (*iradah*),
> decree (*qadar*), destiny (*qada'*), the Book (*kitab*), the permis-
> sion (*idhn*), the appointed time (*ajal*).'

Everything, including all the actions that emanate from a
bondsman, is under these elements and if we deny this we are
removing some of the power of the control of God. He has given
the bondsman his power to act, and to deny the fact that the
bondsman has the ability to act is tantamount to foolishness. It
is a denial of something that we all know — that man can act.

So if somebody acts, he has acted according to his will and
his wish. After the will and the wish, there are destiny and decree,
permission and the Book of God. Everything is within them.

As for the command of God and His prohibitions, they do not
connect with the action of the bondsman in essence. All that
connects with them is the agreement of the bondsman, or his
disagreement regarding that command and prohibitions.

The degree of freedom that the bondsman has is his agreement
or disagreement to follow the decree. This is all. The choice he
has is whether he agrees to follow destiny or not. The more he
is in that agreement, and in that contentment, the more he sees
his destiny.

Imam 'Ali ibn Abi Talib was content with his destiny, which
was that he be martyred. His choice was his recognition of no

choice. The freedom that we imagine is really to be freed of our selves (*nafs*). Indeed the only freedom we have is to recognize completely the non-freedom, which then enables us to see the absolute freedom of the Absolute.

If we are intelligent we obey. If we are not, we are afflicted. The only choice we have is to learn how to unify our actions with our destinies. It is intelligence that gives us those boundaries, for nobody wants to suffer and if we go against our destiny we will suffer shock and disequilibrium instead of the smooth progress we all inherently desire.

However, if the self is to evolve to its full spiritual potential, surrender, purification and enlightenment are necessary stages in the journey. Some people undergo a great deal of hardship and afflictions, while for others the way is easier. Indeed there is a well-known tradition that says: 'It is out of God's love that some people are dragged to the Garden on bleeding knees.' It is also said that 'the Garden is surrounded by fires and the Fire is surrounded by gardens.' One knows how easy it is to be enticed into attractive pleasures and how difficult it is to leave them behind and regain equilibrium.

Imam 'Ali ibn Abi Talib said:

> 'All of this world is ignorance except where knowledge occurs. And all of knowledge is evidence (against you) except what has been acted upon. And all action is vanity except that which is sincere. And sincerity is in danger until the bondsman is given respite with what is going to be his seal (end).'[29]

We are as good as the way in which we end this existence. The condition at the point of departure from this world obviously bears more weight than the actions of earlier times. Therefore, the state of the person, as far as his sincerity and purity are concerned, at the last moments of his life, carries greater significance upon the station of his released soul in the next existence. In the same way, when a child is born into this world, he is marked physically and mentally more by the condition of his mother on the day of his birth, than by her state on any single day in the middle of the gestation period. The mother's condition at the child's birth marks the seal of his birth as his final actions denote the seal of his death.

> It is related from Imam Hasan ibn 'Ali that he was asked about the Saying of Allah, the Exalted:
> 'And We have created everything according to a measure.'

> The Imam said:
> 'He says, Allah, the Exalted, that we have created everything for the people of the fire, according to their actions.'[30]

Every action has an equal and opposite reaction. At the gross physical level, action and reaction are mathematically measurable. Every wrong action will bring about its equivalent in evil on the doer. This is a natural law. However, evil and wrong-doing cannot always be fully quantified by us.

Since creation is based on goodness, good deeds are always related to increase, while bad actions generate an identical degree of negativity. This Saying shows us that the people of the Fire will be punished justly, according to the exact measure (content) of their wrongdoing.

Contentment with the Decree

Imam 'Ali ibn Abi Talib said:

> 'I heard the **Blessed** Prophet say:

> "Allah, the Majestic, said: He, who is not content with My decree and does not believe in My destiny, let him seek a God other than Me." '[31]

The Blessed Prophet also said:

> 'None of you will believe unless he believes in the decree —
> its goodness and badness, its sweetness and bitterness.'[32]

If we do not believe that these laws were set, we will consider them to be sweet or bitter depending upon our reaction to the outcome of events. If we have acted erroneouly, for example, and the laws have come upon us, we will consider them bitter; yet they are there whether we like it or not.

Iman is connected with trust. Trust can be unshakable, when it is founded on knowledge and thereby reliable. The word in Arabic also connects with peace and security, so it is through knowledge and reliablity that we are secure. This state of belief or trust is not possible unless the believer gains the knowledge of the Cause behind all experiences of goodness and evil, sweetness and bitterness.

All of these opposites are recognized within us as a result of certain causes that interact with the individual and bring about these events. Indeed specific events can be desirable at one time but very undersirable under different circumstances. Self recognition of these mechanisms can only develop when insight has deepened and the situation is seen with the eye of unification. *Iman* is ultimately related to the unity between cause and effect, outer and inner, sweet and bitter, and all the other opposites.

This *hadith* is related from Imam 'Ali Zayn al-'Abidin. The Imam said:

> 'I went out until I came to this wall and leant against it, and there was a man wearing two white garments, looking at my face, and he said to me: "O 'Ali Ibn al-Husayn, what is the matter that I see you sad and depressed? Do you grieve of this world? The provisions of Allah are ready for the good and the evil."
>
> I replied:
> "It is not about this that I am sad but it is as you say."
> "Is your sadness about the hereafter? It is a true promise delivered by a compelling King."
>
> I replied:
> "I am not sad about this, but it is as you say."
> "So what then is your sadness for?"

65

I said:
"I am fearful of the plot of Ibn Zubayr."

The man laughed and said:
"O, 'Ali Ibn al-Husayn, have you seen a man who has been fearful of Allah and He had not saved him?"

I said: "No."

"Have you known a man who asked Allah, Glory be to Him, and was not given?"

Then I said:
"No."

And then I looked and there was no one in front of me.'[33]

This is an example of how the mind of even a fully sublimated and surrendered being may get involved with the processes of the world, and the reminder from the world of the unseen that comes to him, to bring back to the state of sublime contentment.

The Imam, even at the height of his worldly pre-occupation, would have no doubt about 'provisions'. His sadness was due to his concern for man's hypocrisy and his capacity for evil. He was afraid of the calamities that man would bring on his fellow men through ignorance. Here again, the voice of Truth reminds the Master that so long as we are aware of the danger, and fear God, we are safe and, whenever we truly ask God for guidance, we will be given it. Once the counsel of the voice had reached the heart of the Imam, it had served its purpose, so it disappeared.

It is related from Imam Ja'far al-Sadiq that one day the Blessed Prophet laughed until his teeth showed, and he said:

'Do you not ask me what causes me to laugh?'

They said:
'Yes, O Prophet of Allah.'

He said:
'I am surprised with the Muslim, for there can be no decree that Allah makes upon him except the good end of his affairs.'[34]

It is related from Imam Ja'far al-Sadiq that Allah has revealed to the Prophet Musa (Moses):

> 'I did not create any creation more loved by me than My believing bondsman and I only afflict him for that which is good for him, and I restore to him what is good for him, and I am more knowledgeable in what makes right his affair. So let him be patient upon My afflictions, and let him be grateful for all that I bestow upon him. Let him be content with My decree. I will then write him amongst those who are confirmers (the near ones with me) if he acts according to what makes Me content and obeys My commands.'[35]

All destinies occur because of the unfoldment of a set of events, interacting in time. The true Muslim sees the perfection and the truth behind the destiny, which he is witnessing. As an individual he may have his expectations and disappointments but, if he is a believer in God's perfect way, and based on his past experiences, he will know that even if the first impact of the outcome is not agreeable, in the end it will be to his benefit.

When the mercy of God is seen as an affliction the remedy lies in patience; for if the person brings himself to a state of true contentment, the likelihood of him seeing the benefit of the situation will be stronger.

It is related from Imam Muhammad al-Baqir that the Prophet Musa said:

> 'Oh my Lord, I am content with Your destiny. You cause the old ones to die and the young ones to continue to live.'
>
> Then the All Majestic God said:
> 'Oh Musa, Are you not content that I am the One who gives provisions and Who is the guarantor.'
>
> The Prophet Musa said:
> 'Yes, my Lord, You are the best of the guardians and the best of guarantors.'[36]

Contentment with God's decree is related to the knowledge

and understanding of the perfect balance and interaction in the physical and non-physical world, for all of these worlds are unified in God's way. The Prophet Musa sees the perfect relationship between cause and effect, the seen and unseen, and with that understanding he declares his complete dependency on God and his contentment with the Provider of all provisions, known and unknown.

Man's *Rizq* (Provision)

It is related from Imam Ja'far al-Sadiq that a man came to him saying:

'By my father and my mother, preach to me good counsel.'

The Imam said:
'If Allah, the Exalted, has made himself responsible for your provisions, why are you concerned? And if sustenance is already apportioned, why then greed? If accountability is true (just) what is collection for? And if replenishment (from Allah, the Exalted) is true, what is miserliness for? And if punishment from Allah, Glory be to Him, is fire, what is disobedience for? And if death is true, then what is pleasurable anticipation for? If all is truly exposed and known to Allah why then deceive? And if Shaytan is your enemy then why be heedless? And if passage along the straight, thin, narrow path is true (on the Day of Reckoning), what is vanity for? And if everything is according to decree and destiny, why grieve? And if this world is being annihilated, why have security in it?'

Rizq is what gives sustenance to the human being. On the physical level it nourishes and sustains the body; at the higher spiritual level it maintains the inner equilibrium, and confirms the certainty of the purpose of this life and the belief in the hereafter.

God's will and objective for His creation is for His created beings to have access to, and knowledge of, the highest possible state, which is the certainty of the hereafter. Access to this state, which is the final fruit of real surrender and submission, is available to a wide spectrum of people. It is not dependent on the degree or quality of their physical *rizq*.

A pious being with no material wealth and an emperor have the same potential access to this provision. Indeed, the less concern and involvement with material provision there is, the more likely there is to be energy for spiritual development. Insecurity concerning provision will only distract the seeker from the true knowledge and experience of faithful surrender with its joy of dependence on Reality. No one is deprived of access to spiritual knowledge except the denier of the all encompassing Mercy. The characteristics of ingratitude and denial shield and isolate the individual, creating a disconnected, egotistical being, wrapped in an arrogant cocoon of self-inflicted darkness.

Once, through insight and the faculty of reasoning and discrimination, we have come to know that every occurrence in this cosmos is according to prescribed laws, we will then know that the outcome we experience is only according to how these laws interact with each other. Every outcome is, therefore, perfectly prescribed. Any personal dissatisfaction arises from our ignorance of all the factors involved. For the intelligent, sincere person these disappointments will turn into the recognition of their misplaced expectations, making for positive rather than negative experiences.

Imam 'Ali ibn Abi Talib has related that the Blessed Prophet said:

> 'O 'Ali, certainty is that you will not be agreeable to anyone who is incurring the wrath of Allah (or is against Allah). And that you do not glorify anyone for what Allah has brought to you, and seek not to fault anyone for what Allah has not brought to you; for provision will not be brought by covetousness, nor will it be repelled by someone's spite or hate. For Allah, by His wisdom and grace, has made ease and joy in certainty and contentment. And

Allah has made sorrow and distress in doubt and displeasure.

There is no poverty worse than ignorance, and no wealth more useful than reason. There is no loneliness more desperate than vanity; no evidence better than counsel; no reason better than acumen; no caution better than stopping at the bounds of what is forbidden; no account as good as goodness of character; no worship as good as reflection. And the pitfall of talk is lying; the pitfall of knowledge is forgetfulness; the pitfall of devotion is coolness; the pitfall of gracefulness is arrogance; the pitfall of courage is transgression; the pitfall of tolerance is putting someone under obligation to you; the pitfall of beauty is infatuation with yourself: and the pitfall of being a man of good standing is pride.'[38]

The Source of all bounty or provision is the One and Only Creator. So, if an expected goodness has not come to us, it is because something has caused its blockage. This is again part of the laws of the Creator. Whatever happens is a proof of the workings of these laws. If there is any blame to be attached it is to the individual, who has misread or misapplied the laws.

The wide meaning of *rizq* is all those experiences which enable us to continue in our overall sustenance. At the lowest physical level it is food, and at the highest level, it is pure awareness and the true submission that leads to inner freedom. So provisions vary from whatever causes us physical well-being to mental harmony. They increase the individual's state of overall health in both the gross and subtle sense.

As far as creation is concerned, man is inherently programmed towards positive expectations of health, well-being, mental harmony and spiritual awareness with their resultant contentment and gratitude. No matter what circumstances the individual is in, it is theoretically feasible for him to attain a state which will make him appreciate creation in its entirety, and thereby render him a true worshipper of his Creator. So the extent to which man is able to realize the provisions God has created for him is based more on his willingness to see and acknowledge, rather than on the extent of his covetousness or anxieties.

The Finality of God's Decree

It is related of the Blessed Prophet that he was heard to say:

> 'Allah has measured all measures before He created the
> heavens and the earth by fifty thousand years.'[39]

In the Arab culture a thousand does not necessarily imply a
specific figure. In this particular context it means a very long
time before creation unfolded, its essential programming was
already apparent. The *hadith* indicates that the laws that govern
how everything moves were made before the physicalization of
what were to be subjected to them. The subtleties (*lata'if*) of the inner
guiding principles or 'programming' were there before the
physicalization of robotic enactment. Indeed we can compare
ourselves to robots, endowed with a facility that enables us to
act within set bounds, and thereby test the laws of decree and
destiny. This small amount of flexibility enables each of us to
ascertain for himself, within that microscale, that the extent of
our possiblities for action lie within the stream of decree and
destiny, and not beyond it.

We are bound. This sensation or experience of free will, our
so-called freedom, is only for us to recognize the fact that there
is no freedom, so that we may move closer and closer experientially to the point of complete harmony with the decree. This
means full efficiency and management, resulting in complete
unison, where our actions and intentions have coincided with
the decree. This is the centre of the storm, where there is no
more movement or agitation, from which springs the continuous
dynamic motion of existence.

The Blessed Prophet was asked about the knowledge of Allah:

> 'He knew and He wished; He willed and He measured;
> He decreed and He judged and began it. Then He made
> come forth what He had decreed. He judged right as what

He had measured and measured (decreed) what He willed. So by His knowledge was His wish and by His wish was the will, and by His will was the measure and by His measure were the destinies (His judgements), and by His destinies was the finality. So knowledge was first, and His desire was second, and His will was third. The measure is upon destiny in order to finalize or seal it.'[40]

God's knowledge of creation preceded the act of creation. Then came the love of the Creator; from that love emanates creation, which can only be sustained and destroyed according to measures and decree. Then came a beginning and a process, and a destiny for what He had decreed and what He had willed. These are based on measures, and His desire was by His knowledge, and His will was by His desire, and His measures were by His will, and according to His measures is His decree, and according to His decree was the execution.

So His knowledge was first and foremost, and before His desire. His desire came second and His will third. All measures apply to all His decrees by the process of executing that decree. Thus the process starts from the sublime and subtle knowledge and ends with the physical manifestation and interlinking material realities, and the laws that govern them in the causal chain.

The following *hadith* is found in Sahih Muslim in the section on Decree.

Someone came to the Blessed Prophet and said:
'O Prophet of Allah, show us our *din* (religion, life transaction) as though we have been created now. What are we to do today? Is it according to how the pen has dried up, or according to what Allah's *qadar* (measure) has been or is it according to what is going to come to us in future?'

The Blessed Prophet answered:
'It is according to what the pen has dried up with and according to what the measures will dictate (according to what the decree will dictate).'

The man said:
'And how do we act?'

The Blessed Prophet said:
'Act, for everything will flow (emanate) in ease for what
it has been created for, and for everyone his actions will
accordingly be.'[41]

The Blessed Prophet said the pen has dried, it is already done,
and it will unfold according to the decree. So he has shown us
the awesome solidity of the decree's foundations and source,
while at the same time he has encouraged us to act. We are told
that everyone has been given the path of ease for which he has
been created. This means that all of us in whatever situation we
are in seek the equilibrium for which we have been created. It
is decreed that we all seek that which is conducive, and try to
achieve a balance within the constrictions of this life. Man is not
forced by his Creator to be in line with the decree, instead he is
given the opportunity to see his own destiny unfold within the
framework of God's preordained decree.

The Blessed Prophet was asked:

'Are we in a situation in which the affair has been completed
or in an affair that is being reviewed?'

The Blessed Prophet answered:
'We are in an affair that has been completed and we are in
an affair that is being reviewed and revised constantly.'[42]

As far as God is concerned the affair is finished with, because
God is beyond time. Therefore, the Source of all creation is from
non-time and in non-time the question of an action beginning
and ending does not arise. It is zero end. Beginning and end
only exist in the creational and physical realities, so it is only
for us that there is a beginning and an end in a constantly
reviewable situation.

It is related from Imam Ja'far al-Sadiq that Imam 'Ali ibn
Abi Talib said:

'Known for sure that Allah has not given to his bondsman
even though he strives strongly and even though the ways

73

of the bondsman are great and even though his struggling is increased so that he will overcome that which has been written for him in the wise decree, nor will he fall between the weak bondsman and the bondsman's inabilities to reach what has been decreed for him in the Divine Decree.'[43]

The Blessed Prophet is reported to have said:

'Know for sure that if the entire *Ummah* (community of believers) has gathered in order to benefit you by something, they cannot benefit you by anything unless Allah has written it for you; and if all of them have been collected to cause you an evil act they cannot cause you a loss or evil act except according to what has been written by Allah. The pens have been lifted and the ink is dry.'[44]

Say: Nothing will afflict us save what Allah has ordained for us; He is our Patron and on Allah let the believers rely.

(9:51)

If the final decree of God has been executed there is no way of overcoming it. Whatever entities have been created are under the influence of their natures, which may be guided or misguided. The selves are under the influences of the *'uqul*. All of the small individual *'uqul* are under the original *'Aql*, the One God.

Another way of looking at this is to say that everything on this earth is under the heavenly influences, according to the decree of God. All the heavenly influences are under the *Malakut*, and the *Malakut* is enslaved by the *Jabarut*. The *Jabarut* is under the command of the *Jabbar*, Who is the enforcer for all His creation. Hence there is no possiblity of any trace in existence except by His power. There is no doer save Him, and the entire earth is in His hands. The entire heavens are folded in His right hand, and the moon, the sun and the stars are all according to His command.

Surely I rely on Allah, my Lord and your Lord; there is

no living creature but He holds it by its forelock... .

(11:56)

And Allah has created you and what you make.

(37:96)

The Purpose of Creation

People came to Imam Hasan ibn 'Ali after the death of his father, Imam 'Ali ibn Abi Talib, to pay him allegiance.

> Imam Hasan said:
> 'Glory to be He Who has decreed His order and has selected those whom he preferred and has made His order to encompass it and has bestowed well-being. I glorify Him in a way that He can complete His bounty (delights) upon us, and thereby deserve His contentment.
> 'This world is the abode of. affliction and plots, and whatever is in it is in descendance. Allah has informed us as to how we may heed it. He put forth to us His warnings so that there is no excuse for us after having been warned. So hold on to austerity with that which is being annihilated and have desire for that which will remain, and fear Allah in private and in public.
> ' 'Ali, in his life and in his death and in his resurrection, lived according to the decree and died according. to his destiny.
> 'I accept your allegiance (promise) on condition that you be at peace with whomever I am at peace with, and you be against whom I am against.'
> They all paid allegiance to him.[45]

In this tradition, the Imam glorifies the Source of all creation, and explains the function of man's experience in this world; which is the growth of his faculty of discrimination so that, being warned, he seeks that which is permanent, taking continuous precaution against transgression.

Imam Hasan testifies to the perfection of Imam 'Ali ibn Abi Talib's life, which was lived in accordance with the decree, and in fulfilment of his destiny. He then accepts the allegiance of the people on the condition that they follow his judgements. This will save them from the turmoils and afflictions of this life, and give them the opportunity of true surrender and awakening to the high station that God has ordained for man.

The following Saying is reported by more than one Imam.

> A man from the people of Iraq entered to Imam 'Ali ibn Abi Talib, because he had been asked to come out and fight against Mu'awiyah, and said:
> 'Tell us about our coming out against the people of Syria, is it by Allah's decree and destiny?'
> Imam 'Ali said to him:
> 'Yes, old man. By Allah, you do not go up a hillock, nor do you go inside the valley, unless it is by decree and destiny from Allah.'
> The man then said:
> 'Then to Allah I account for my difficulties?'
> The Imam said:
> 'Slowly, old man; maybe you are thinking that destiny is inevitable and that decree is essential. If it was like that, chastisement and reward will be nullified; order, prohibition and admonishment would be meaningless; and the meaning of promise and threat will fall; and there will be no blame upon a man of evil action nor any praise for one of good action. In fact, the one of good action is more blameworthy than the one who commits sins and the one who commits sins is more worthy of goodness than the one who commits good action. This is the saying of the worshippers of idols and enemies of the Merciful, and of the faction of the people who believe in pre-determination, and the Magians.'[46]

Earlier on we were told that decree and action are like soul (*ruh*) and body (*jasad*). One cannot experience the soul unless one has a body. Body is one's action, while one's soul is the decree. It is the subtle power that makes one able to act. One cannot exist without the other. Decree is meaningless unless one acts. So decree is the outcome of one's action as it is experienced.

If one's action has been selfless, or has been about true worship and adoration, the outcome is perfection.

The Imam continued:

'O old man, Allah, the Exalted, has obligated with choice and prohibited with warning, and has given much upon little. And Allah will not be disobeyed in defeat, and He will not be obeyed forcibly.'[46]

God has given his bondsmen the choice of either recognizing their slavehood or not. He does not like to be obeyed forcibly. His *Sunnah* is based on love, generosity and mercy. The animals are created without will, and they obey the laws of their nature. So why did God create this higher being man, with will, if it were not to give him the choice of recognizing His glory?

The Imam further continued:

'He did not create the heavens and the earth and what is between them in vain. This is the imagination of those who deny. Woe to those who deny, from the Fire.'

The old man then got up and burst out into poetry:
'You are the Imam whom we hope to be able to ask on the Day of Salvation when we expect forgiveness from the Merciful. You have cleared for us from our *din* what was perplexing. May your God reward you for all your good-liness. We now have no excuse in committing any vice.'[46]

According to another tradition, Imam 'Ali also told the man:

'The affair (command) is from Allah and so is the judge-ment (destiny).'

Then the Imam recited the following *ayah* from the Qur'an:

'Your Lord has ordained that you do not worship except Him and be goodly to your parents.'[46]

Decree and Destiny, the Secret of God

An important tradition is related from Imam 'Ali ibn Abi Talib, which contains the key to understanding the whole question of decree and destiny. This is diving into the sea that he adivsed a man, in an earlier quoted *hadith*, not to enter.

> 'For certainly decree is a secret of the secret of Allah, and a veil of Allah's veil, a preserved sanctuary of Allah lifted up in the veil of Allah, folded up from the creation of Allah, sealed by the seal of Allah earlier on in the knowledge of Allah.
>
> 'Allah has unburdened His slaves from its knowledge [the entire knowledge of the decree] and lifted it up beyond their witnessing and the extent of their comprehension, because they will not reach it by the knowledge of lordship, nor by the capability of everlastingness, nor by the might of illumination, nor by the power of unification, because it is a pure and abounding sea that is Allah's. Its depth is what is between the heavens and the earth; its breadth engulfs what is between the east and the west. Black like the darkest night, full of serpents and reptiles, it rises sometimes and subsides at others. At the bottom of it there is a shining sun which no one is allowed to be exposed to except the One Solitary God, the One and Only. For he who dwells upon it and looks at it opposes Allah in His wisdom and competes with Him in His power. Lifting up His veil and revealing Allah's secrets brings forth the anger of Allah and (whoever does this) his abode will be hell and the worst of outcomes.'[47]

The term decree (measure) here indicates all the laws — known and unknown. Many of them will be discovered by us as our intellect grows in discrimination, while others are of such subtlety that they will remain veiled from us. Our exposure to these aspects of knowledge is very limited, which gives us a measure of protection and relative security. The knowledge, which is available to creation, is what is relevant to this existence, which is in time, and therefore limited and contained.

The ultimate truth or Divine knowledge, which is timeless, is shown here to be like an ocean wave, whose depth is the distance between the heavens and the earth, and whose breadth is between sunrise and sunset; for this infinite ocean of knowledge encompasses all experiences and all realities. When it is looked at through man's vision, which is subject to the limitations of time, the dynamism of this ocean is so bewildering that its true meaning will elude him, as the totality of this vast truth can only be grasped by God, the One and Only. Therefore, the more the mortal being examines and reflects upon decree and destiny, the more he is bewildered; the deeper he goes, the more he will be subject to confusion.

His questions can only be resolved through subjective and experiential application, for intellectual knowledge of this phenomenon tends merely to bring out new issues, which further agitate the mind. The final solution comes when the separation between the individual and his final Cause ceases and a unific state of beingness arises. In this state the individual experiences an instantaneous and harmonized connection between all causes and effects, and lives within a unified field of beingness. He is then simultaneously aware of the ripples of the waves and the calm of the ocean below. When he was seeking the knowledge of decree and destiny he was affected by the waves, although he had some knowledge of the infinite ocean below. However, when he awakes to the unific state, he is both in the infinite non-changing ocean and the ever-changing waves at the same times. He acknowledges both and sees they are one.

Until the individual attains this state of union, the correct courtesy is to approach whatever situation in which he finds himself in a state of awareness and to surrender fully to the flow of events. Similarly, for the person who is exploring the shores of an ocean, the correct courtesy is for him to connect fully with the bounds of the ocean and its surface, until such time as the wave beckons him in. Then he will swim and explore, until he internalizes more knowledge. This enables him to dive further out without risk to himself. If he is in this state of awareness, he will know the time he has to care for his physical body, and the time he may dive into the inner ocean. For everything there is a time; a time to remain on the shore and a time to walk on the ocean. The real courtesy is to know the state one is in at each specific moment and be fully at one with that state.

Imam 'Ali ibn Abi Talib says the hearts go through different states. Sometimes they are open; during those times one can worship and concentrate on inner development. At other times they are closed and one restricts oneself to the basic duties. The key lies in contentment with whatever state one finds oneself in; for then one is already submerged in the total ocean of submission.

4

Selected Topics Relating to Decree and Destiny

Introduction

The purpose of the discussions in the preceding chapters, which were based on Qur'an and *hadith*, was for each one of us to reflect upon how often we have gone against the decree and suffered in consequence. When this has happened we have suspected that God's judgement or destiny was either wrong or we were afflicted by bad luck.

This assumption is inaccurate although appealing. There is always a tendency to blame an outside agency and to fail to realize that there is no outside or inside, for all creations are intertwined and influenced by each other. Yet we can only discern Reality's perfection if we recognize our own imperfections, which arise from our arrogance, expectations and whims.

In order to expand on our earlier analysis in relation to the existence that encompasses us all, we shall discuss the following series of concepts.

Determinism

Every aspect of creation, known or unknown, is subject to a predetermined pattern — ie, to laws and regulations that build up to a climax until the point when the aspect in question, be it a human form or a planetary cosmos, is recycled.

The human soul is brought about in conjunction with the physical form of the body and its faculties of discrimination. When the body is discarded at the point of death, the soul carries on into the non-time zone — ie, forever. The manifestations of all these entities stem from a Reality, that is, beyond time. Yet we, as individuals, experience everything in this existence *in time*. Our experiences in this world have unfolded in an interactional manner between our wills and desires, and the world around us. Therefore we have always had a manner of free will and have been a party to our destiny.

However, from the point of view of the Creator of all, Who is beyond the laws of time, the meaning of everything that occurs *in time* is predetermined and pre-known. The Creator's laws are going to unfold in an interactional manner and their result will only be known to us as we interact with them. So it is not really relevant to us as we journey through this life that God, Who is beyond time, knows the final outcome of our actions in the absolute sense. Actions which are for us still unfolding in time will be appropriately punished or rewarded according to the extent of our compliance with the universal laws.

The creational laws are referred to in the following *ayah*:

> No evil befalls on the earth nor in your own souls, but it
> is in a book before We bring it into existence; surely that
> is easy for Allah.
>
> (57:22)

The reference to "in a book" is not meant in a fatalistic sense but from the angle of cause and effect. Every evil like any other occurrence has a cause. Like all other causes and effects it has a beginning and an end and it is subject to the laws that govern it. These laws are in the creational book.

The predetermined knowledge of God is referred to in this *ayah*:

> And with Him are the keys of the unseen treasures —
> none knows them but He; and He knows what is in the
> land and the sea; and there falls not a leaf but He knows
> it; nor a grain in the darkness of the earth, nor anything
> green nor dry but (it is all) in a clear book.
>
> (6:59)

82

This means that when the time is ripe, the leaf will dry up and the molecule split. The knowledge of this is in the chromosomes, programmed inherently in the tree. It is this knowledge that is with God. God does not sit with a telescope saying: "Now I am going to let this leaf fall." Nor equally does He say: "I am going to afflict that fellow, he deserves it." God is beyond time. You and I are in time. It is important for us to feel the existential dynamism of this world, so we do not exceed the limits and over-reach ourselves. Afflictions are only the mercy of nature teaching us how to obey the rules of life.

The "clear Book" referred to in the above *ayah* is not the physical Qur'an in our hands. It is the Book of Reality. The Qur'an is a description and a manifestation of the Book of Reality. All manifest things are encompassed by the One and Only Reality. Everything is written in the book of *non-time* to be experienced *in* time. There is only God, and wherever one turns is the face of God.

Imam 'Ali ibn Abi Talib has said: 'And you are the evident book', meaning whatever you can experience is according to the Book. If you have acted in harmony with the laws and measures of the decree, your destiny will be contentment. If you have moved in the other direction, you will also experience the mercy of God through your afflictions. Whenever trouble afflicts you, a specific door will be closed to you, so that you will be forced to move to where there is an opening. This is not to punish you. It is God's natural way to guide His creation.

Certainty and Change

There are certain laws that are not possible to change. We cannot, for example, change death. It is absolute and fixed. We can only defy death before it arrives. We may defy nature, but our defiance is within the limits and bounds of the laws that govern nature.

If the temperature drops below thirty-two degrees Fahrenheit, water will freeze. We cannot change the natural phenomenon of freezing, but we can bring that ice indoors and melt it, or increase the atmospheric pressure upon water and thereby reduce the temperature at which it freezes. This example illustrates that, although we cannot negate or escape Reality's laws, we can work within them.

A wise father, who realizes the pugnacious nature of his son, will know that he cannot change his temperament. He can, however, put his combative nature to good use by encouraging him to fight evil for the sake of humanity; otherwise, the son's aggression will be manifested indiscriminately.

From God's standpoint everything is certain. This is the meaning of saying that everything is written in the Book of Destiny. The greater the man's ignorance, the more he will believe he can change the situation. The closer we move to the knowledge of Reality, the more we know that everything is certain. The less freedom we have, the less choice there is. The closer we are to certainty, the less we can talk about change.

Change is existential and superficial. Certainty is absolute and concerned with the inner. Change has to do with Divine laws (*Shari'ah*), certainty with Reality (*Haqiqah*). According to *Shari'ah* man must constantly strive to change for the better. This is the meaning of moving from one decree to another. This is change within bounds.

When we strive to improve our destiny we must face the limits of freedom and interact with it to the best of our ability, realistically rather than romantically.

Certainty and change are two facets emanating from one Source. We cannot experience one without the other. We cannot experience time, which is change, unless there is an understanding of non-change. Change is within certainty. Its boundary is certainty, and eventually it will reach a point of certainty.

The following *ayah* illustrates how the foundation of certainty and change is from one Source:

And when My servants ask you concerning Me, then surely

I am very near; I answer the prayer of the supplicant when
he calls on Me, so they should answer My call and believe
in Me that they may walk in the right way.

(2:186)

Reality, the cause of both the fixed and unfixed, of certainty
and change, and the access to it, is within us. We have to go
beyond the fixed and the unfixed to That from Which certainty
and change have emanated. This is the meaning of 'Call for
God, ask for God'.

We notice that an apparent conflict is natural in creation. On
the one hand life is experienced in dynamic flux, yet we, as
human beings, constantly look for certainty. This apparent conflict can only be resolved according to what has already been
described. The body and the physical world are in change and
uncertainty, yet our soul or self is, in essence, of a certain and
unchanging nature. If we look within, we reach the fundamental
abode of total security and timeless certainty — a divine attribute. The more we look outwardly, the more we see uncertainty;
for certainty cannot exist in the outer world except in dynamic
flux.

There is an absolute decree that we will die, and there is a
relative decree that the length of our lifetime is dependent on
whether we abuse our system or not. The average life span for
man is about seventy years. We can live out that measure or,
through the adverse effects of transgressing the bounds of good
health, through ignorance, we will shorten our life span.

It is recorded in al-Majlisi's *Bihar al-Anwar*, Volume V, that
Imam Ja'far al-Sadiq has said:

> 'Those who die because of their sins (transgressions) are
> more than those who die because of their destiny. And
> those who live because of their goodly actions are more
> than those who have lived because of their allotted life.'[48]

It is not unusual to see men of true abandonment living to a
ripe old age of ninety or a hundred years. They may also die

young. What was there for Sayyida Fatima Zahra to live for
after the death of the Blessed Prophet other than to witness the
betrayal of his teachings? By then, in any case, she had seen the
nature and treachery of this world and she had known the nature
of Divine Reality and longed for it.

The question of the possible postponement of a destiny such
as death is explained in the following *hadith qudsi* (Divinely revealed tradition):

> 'He who belittles one of My lovers (saints) is contesting
> with Me in a battle and I am never so hesitant in anything
> I do as when I hesitate in taking the life of a *mu'min*
> (believer), and I hate to cause him what he thinks is
> against him, but it is unavoidable.'[49]

Through this and similar traditions we learn the meaning
behind the reference to the 'hesitancy' of God in relation to the
death of His believing bondsmen. One of God's attributes is the
Eternal or the Everlasting and the believer, who adores God and
His attributes, loves eternity. Life on this planet is not eternal
but its seizure gives the impression of a breakdown of a desirable
eternal state. The so-called 'hesitancy' of God to take the life of
the believer merely reflects the believer's probable reluctance to
leave the known, and go through the state of transformative
confusion that will follow death.

Destiny is the experienced outcome of events; in the case of
life, man's destiny is death. There is an average term of life
which changes according to inherited physical traits as well as
natural environmental situations. In addition to these factors
the person himself can play a crucial part in shortening or pro-
longing the allotted term because the person is an integrated
part of the final outcome of the destiny or allotted term.

The knowledge of God, the Exalted, encompasses all acts and
experiences all happenings, for He is beyond time. Thus the
allotted term of a man's life is only known to God; so far as the
individual is concerned it will only be known when it occurs.
This occurrence will come about partly by his own doing and

the extent of his connectedness.

God, Who loves His bondsmen, is hesitant (so to speak) to break the faithful bondsman's illusion of on-goingness in this world. The bondsman is correct to believe in and desire perpetuity, but this does not belong to this world. Therefore death is inevitable.

Cause and Effect

Consider a man who has created a playground, and allows people the freedom to play in it. A variety of outcomes will arise from their activities. The specific activities of the players are not determined; the interlinks or the causes and effects that govern this playground are. It is not determined, for example, that a man will be riding a swing and he will fall and break his neck. What is determined is what will occur if he swings too high — that he will lose his balance, slip off the swing and fall. We have freedom to decide whether we use swings, and the manner in which we interact with them. The knowledge that is with God is the knowledge of the laws that govern these swings. These laws are perpetual. It is we who are transitory, moving in and out of the swings of the amusement park of life.

If we look at everything in this existence from the point of view that they are under the knowledge of God, by the knowledge of God, according to the laws of God, then everything that exists is under the decree of God, including human existence. However, if we regard everything from the viewpoint of limitation — that is, according to time and place — the situation is then somewhat different. It is also according to the decree but we are part of the decree. It is here that cause and effect come into play, in the realm of spontaneous interaction, where we can both be the cause of an event and affected by its effect. It is in this arena of 'personality' that we have 'affliction' and the lack of it. It is in the interaction between cause and effect that we taste the Fire and the Garden. One cause gives birth to an effect and that effect gives birth to another cause. We interact with this in a tangential manner. This is the process of upbringing, through which man achieves his potential.

Thus, cause and effect are the ways the Creator brings us up to our full potential of complete abandonment and *true*, rather than *questioned*, submission — so that we may move with the knowledge in the now, not in the experiential knowledge of yesterday or tomorrow. Nevertheless, these too are important.

The sensitive observation of the interaction of cause and effect, and its relationship with us, brings about wisdom and maturity. However, we are not always in a state of faith, and we are given the opportunity of committing the same errors again and again until we either learn from them or go in ignorance to our graves.

In this causal chain with its multitudinous, superimposed events, the destiny of the individual is affected by others. If, for example, the majority of the population abuse the environment, the land will become barren, whether we are in prayer day and night or not. If we have abused nature through excessive use of fertilizers and pesticides, no matter how well-meaning and good-hearted we are, a time will come when we will starve because of our abuse of the land. Equally if we have wisdom, like the Prophet Nuh (Noah), a time will come when we realize that all of our warnings are not going to change society and affliction will come to it through its own deeds. When the Prophet Nuh realized that his people would not heed his warnings and change their ways, and hence that natural calamities were inevitable, he built his ark and sailed away on it to safety.

However, most of us believe that the afflictions that come to us through man's acts of injustice are the afflictions of God. This is our stupidity. Everything is from God, therefore overall punishment as such is a creation of God, but injustice is what we bring about by our doing. Man can punish in revenge and anger. We should not confuse this with Divine punishment.

Therefore, from an existential or humanistic point of view, we cannot separate the material from the moral. We cannot separate somebody else's actions from our action, and from the situation we find ourselves in. We cannot separate our home from our neighbour's, our family from society. They are all interconnected, and they will all affect each other. There is no escape. The only difference is the extent of this effect and its influence.

Choice within Bounds

The More the Knowledge, the Less the Choice

The ultimate freedom is that of no-choice, for were we to be aware of and consider every factor of a given situation, we would discover there to be only one optimum (most efficient) way in which we could act, although the momentary consequences of this action might not seem desirable at the time.

Take, for example, the question of choosing a career. A person has many desires, strengths and limitations as well as dislikes and if all of these factors are known, an order of hierarchy will emerge. Then this model will be matched with the situation in the world at large and, if all of this has been logically pursued and no factors are left out, the best career path will emerge, leaving no room for further choice. The more confused we are about the different variables that enter this model, the more supposed choices we will end up with. However, the more clearly the objectives are defined and the parameters and variables are known, the less will be the choice of the course of action open to us.

To take another example, if a person is restricted by illness the more severe those restrictions are, the less the choice of food that is available to him. We may conclude, therefore, that apparent choice and freedom is greater when there are more unknowns and variables in the system than vice versa. Therefore, the more knowledge we acquire of any situation, be it simple or complex, the more defined and specific will be the appropriate or necessary line of action.

Freedom within the Decree

The following *ayat* indicate that there is a measure of freedom for us to act within the decree. Indeed, if we move along the decree within its laws, we will see their perfection and nothing will afflict us.

> Whoever desires this present life, We hasten to him therein what We please for whomsoever We desire, then We assign to him the hell; he shall enter it despised, driven away.
> And whoever desires the hereafter and strives for it as he ought to strive and he is a believer; (as for) these, their striving shall surely be accepted.
> All do We aid — these as well as those — out of the bounty of your Lord, and the bounty of your Lord is not confined.
>
> (17:18–20)

> And Allah sets forth a parable: (Consider) a town safe and secure to which its means of subsistence come in abundance from every quarter; but it became ungrateful for Allah's favours, therefore Allah made it to taste the utmost degree of hunger and fear because of what they wrought.
>
> (16:112)

> ...and it did not beseem Allah that He should be unjust to them, but they were unjust to their own souls.
>
> (29:40)

> Whoever does good, it is for his own soul, and whoever does evil, it is against it; and your Lord is not in the least unjust to the servants.
>
> (41:46)

> My word shall not be changed, nor am I in the least unjust to the bondsmen.
>
> (50:29)

> Surely we have shown him the way (the real way is clear); he may be grateful or ungrateful.
>
> (76:3)

One meaning of the last *ayah* is that the way or path of freedom is laid out for us but, if we close our eyes, we do not see it. If we are attached or enslaved to something else, we cannot see that the freedom is within us.

The Importance of Gratitude

We enter into the path of freedom through the gate of gratitude. Gratitude renders the heart empty and clear. When we are in a state of thankfulness, there is no attachment at that moment, because the heart has already detached itself from whatever it was attached to, by the fact of that gratitude. This is the way of freedom. If we deny this, we will remain enslaved by one self-inflicted chain after another.

> And when your Lord made it known: If you are ungrateful,
> I would certainly give to you more, and if you are ungrate-
> ful, My chastisement is truly severe.
>
> (14:7)

This *ayah* means that the growth of faith and certainty will enable the individual to see more directly the cause of every event. He will then see nothing other than the manifestation of the all connecting fibre of Reality, with subtle and gross multi-di-mensional layers interacting upon each other in dynamic flux.

Man's Interaction with the Decree

> Corruption has appeared in the land and the sea on ac-
> count of what the hands of men have wrought, that He
> may make them taste of that which they have done, so
> that they may return.
>
> (30:41)

The laws that govern the existence of this world are neutral in that fire will burn a good man, if he plunges his hand in it, in the same way it will burn an evil man. It is through our deeds that we make these laws benign and healthy, or corrupt and deranged. God has given us the potential to see how our actions are manifested in this world, either positively or negatively. This is the meaning of the Garden or the Fire. So we choose the entry, and we forget the key to heaven or hell experientially here and now, by what we earn with our hands. We have the possibility of both. As Muhyi al-Din ibn 'Arabi said: 'When the veil is lifted, it will be seen that a man sends himself to the Garden or sends himself to the Fire.'

> Whoever desires the gain of the hereafter, We will give him more of that gain; and whoever desires the gain of this world, We give him of it, and in the hereafter he has no portion.
>
> (42:20)

We cannot have total gratification within the physical and biological bonds in this world, for there is a limit to our energy. We cannot simultaneously pursue the shortlived pleasures of this world and those of the next, because there is only one heart. There is a *hadith* that says: 'God has not put in the breast of man more than one heart.' We will get what we pursue, for we are not separate from the total Reality.

Knowledge of the Limits

The *ayat* quoted in the last section describe how the degree of our freedom lies within set bounds. Freedom is defined as how we confront these limitations. Our body has certain limitations as far as physical and intellectual achievement is concerned, for example. There is a limit as to how much we can sleep or eat or walk. All systems function within limits and these limits are the safeguards of creation against the disruptions and ignorance of man.

The Creator in His infinite wisdom gives men a chance to participate in learning about the systems that govern existence, adopting and adhering to their laws. The quicker we apply these laws consciously, the smoother will be our integration and the deeper our knowledge of the unifying factors.

We are created in order to respect these limitations and appreciate their wisdom and value. We are given an insight through them into the limitless Reality from which these limits have emanated. Access to the limitlessness of the King and His infinite chamber comes only after we have travelled through the narrow corridors of the palace, waited politely and contentedly in the antechambers (respecting the limits) for permission to enter His presence. The King was always there and in full control but we did not know it.

Only when we acknowledge this fact and explain it in our limited sphere will we begin to comprehend something of the Limitless; for the Creator has given us a certain degree of freedom within these limits in order that we may be trained through controlled participation in His perfect creational plan.

It has been said earlier in this book that there are certain situations that are completely determined. It is determined, for example, that we are going to die eventually or that we need sustenance. All the laws of Reality, such as gravity, electromagnetism, thermodynamics etc, are determined. Equally it is determinied that we desire peace. Every human being loves peace; even those who enjoy noise would soon crave peace and rest were they to be subjected to loud music for a prolonged period of time.

Certain sets of conditions may arise that have, according to the laws that govern them, become so non-conducive to our well-being that we abandon them. We can leave a piece of land that has been abused, and move into virgin ground. The generosity of nature is such that we can do this again and again until finally a limit is reached, when destruction on a mass scale begins to take place.

There is a limit as to how much we can rejuvenate our own system. If we abuse our body, a time will come when it may take years for the cells to rejuvenate. Equally a time may come when the body has deteriorated to such an extent that it has gone beyond the possibility of rejuvenation.

Man's Choice

The choice that is given to man is determined but not in its finality. What is determined is that man is given a choice to be either satanic or merciful. It has also been determined that certain actions will bring about certain results. However, it is not determined that a certain individual on a Thursday in May will overeat at lunch, and suffer from a stomach ache. What is determined is that overtaxing the digestive system will ultimately cause physical collapse and illness.

If man had not been given some margin of choice, he would not have had the possibility of being able to discover his Creator. We, as humans, have consciousness and are subject to temptation and affliction, and we have to act. This is the meaning of 'choice within bounds'.

Disappointment or Punishment, an Indicator of Wrong or Inappropriate Action

The question of punishment is referred to in the following *ayah*:

> Say: O Allah, Master of the Kingdom! Thou givest the kingdom to whomsoever Thou pleasest and takest away the kingdom from whomsoever Thou pleasest, and Thou exaltest whom Thou pleasest and abasest whom Thou pleasest; in Thine hand is the good; surely, Thou hast power over all things.
>
> (3:26)

It is not determined beforehand that a person is going to be humiliated or debased. Humiliation is an aspect of total justice. If the person puts himself in a position that brings about abasement, humiliation is bound to come to him as the result. However, everything ultimately is caused by the Power that has brought about this creation and all its laws.

> ...Say: All is from Allah... .
>
> (4:78)

The next *ayah* explains how we have choice, yet at the same time we are bound:

> And as to Thamud, We showed them the right way, but they chose error above guidance, so there overtook them the scourge of an abasing chastisement for what they earned.
>
> (41:17)

Everybody has been guided because we all contain the Guide within us but, if we refuse to abandon our egos, we will blame someone else and carry on in a state of blindness. God will not change the bounds that He has set for His creation; those living within the bounds must first change themselves.

> This is because Allah has never changed a favour which He has conferred upon a people until they change their own condition; and because Allah is Hearing, Knowing.
>
> (8:53)

Change does not necessarily come about by our cognition of the need for it; action must also take place. To give a possible example, a man who had previously been mean becomes generous; as a result his existential wealth may then have increased, because people who are generous often attract wealth.

The Freedom of No Choice

The so-called freedom of choice is based on confusion and is a result of not knowing our objective and the parameters involved, because if we knew these there would be one choice.

The ultimate choice of a path is that which does not confront us with any possibility of multiple choices, so it frees us from that process of choosing and selecting, which contains within it the possibility of mistakenly not selecting the optimum choice.

When individualized and egotistic choice has been abandoned, the natural choice will be selected and there will be continuous, harmonious flow.

Collective Destiny

Destiny for an individual is his interaction with the decree and experience of the outcome of it. The same applies to individuals who have a link with each other such as a family, a tribe, or a nation. The stronger the interlink among its people, the closer the individual destiny is to the collective destiny.

In the same way that an individual will live out his ongoing destiny, and ultimately his final destiny — the experience of death — so will all the members of a group or nation, who have a common denominator or bond amongst themselves. The collective destiny of a society or a community is the outcome of the interaction of its people's will with the decree. The gap between an individual destiny and a collective destiny is only as wide as the separation between the direction of the individual and the direction of the collective.

In the case of the Prophet Nuh, he lived amongst transgressors whose long term wrong actions were the cause of major natural phenomena such as earthquakes and floods. The Prophet Nuh exhorted his people to reverse the course of their behaviour in the hope of averting these disasters. When he realized that their will was to continue in their old pattern, thus sealing the inevitability of the catastrophe, he constructed the Ark which enabled him to escape their doom.

The Blessed Prophet, as a man of abandonment and submission, will have always maintained his state of inner contentment despite the outer turmoil that may have been surrounding him. Confirmed in his state of inner certainty, he would not have been concerned about the outcome of events, but as a human being he would maintain some concern about this body because this is the law of physical reality. Even if he was inwardly in a state of wishing to abandon his body, being who he was and knowing what he knew, he would still act as a guardian of the body and do his best to care for it, because he could not claim that it was his.

He will have been content with whatever state he was in, for he recognized the perfect beauty of the laws of the Creator as they related to himself and the people around him. These laws will never change. This is the secret of certainty in the people of belief and knowledge. If one is out of the way of the radiation beam, it will not affect one but, if one is in its path one will be affected by it. Even the most perfect being cannot escape the perfect consistency of God's laws.

As the entire creation stems from one Creator, and is moving along a direction in time, there is an interdependency among all elements of this creational fibre. Every individual will affect the collective will to varying degrees of intensity, although the impact may be so minute or subtle that we are unaware of its significance.

This is the meaning behind the saying that the influence of an awakened soul is cosmic. The reverse is also true. One rotten apple can eventually spoil the entire basket.

The individual can choose, within certain bounds, to rise high or sink to the lowest depths. This is the same choice that faces societies or nations as groups. Whoever is within a particular society or nation will be affected by the behaviour of the majority.

The ignorant person tries to save himself by minimizing the impact of undesirable outer events upon himself. The man of knowledge will translate his desire for safety and well-being into positive action in order to influence the others towards knowledge, and thereby correct their behaviour. This path may appear more arduous but it is the only path. The man of knowledge sees only one Cause and one underlying Foundation for all existence. Thus, he sees no escape from fulfilling the cause of his existence, which is to know his Creator, adore, praise and worship Him.

In the case of the Prophet Musa, the wrong actions of his people resulted in numerous catastrophes which afflicted both the Prophet and his people.

During the Battle of Uhud the Blessed Prophet suffered severe wounds due to the disobedience of some of his followers. His counsel from the beginning had been that the battle was not to be fought from outside the town. However, his followers were over-confident, remembering their success at the earlier battle, in which they had overcome an enemy who had been superior both in equipment and in number. The Blessed Prophet finally conceded to the wish of the majority on the condition that they did not abandon their position in the field. He planned the distribution of the forces but, as soon as there was a break in the enemy rank, the flanks of the Muslims disintegrated. Some people ran after the booty believing, because of their expectations, that an easy victory had been achieved.

The Blessed Prophet was well aware of his people's weaknesses both in terms of spiritual stamina and adherence to discipline. He was aware that this lesson would ultimately be of benefit but at the same time it nearly spelled disaster. He himself was instrumental in teaching them the lesson, because he was badly wounded; so in this case the teacher was the blackboard upon which the story was written with blood and arrows.

Revealed and Acquired Knowledge

Facts and information are realities whose relevance and importance change from time to time and from circumstance to circumstance. If a man is pursuing a commercial enterprise, for example, and he is given the information that there is need for a specific commodity in a certain town, this knowledge is so significant and urgent to the achievement of that objective that he endeavours to conceal the fact. If, however, he has no business involvement with that commodity or that town, the fact is useless. Hence facts are as good as their usability. This usability is as good as the network of knowledge of the person who uses them.

As a person grows in knowledge through experience, that knowledge becomes like a net in which he catches the information which impinges on it. These facts and information impinge on multi-dimensional nets, which are based on the past experiences he has stored in his mind. As each specific input touches his mind, it will activate a certain part of that net.

These personally acquired aspects of knowledge have their relevance and priorities according to circumstances. While a man is trying to find a path through a wood, for example, the knowledge of Mozart's music is of no use to him. Equally an innate system of priority knowledge will enable him to identify what information should be used at what time. He is swimming because he knows the exercise is beneficial to his body, when suddenly he receives a message that his child has been badly hurt in the house. He jumps out of the pool and runs in to help the child. The child's need takes precedence over the potential physical benefits of exercise.

This is the way we live; we assimilate facts and information into a network of knowledge, which is based on our experiences, and we act accordingly. This is human information on existential facts. Its value scale changes from time to time, from culture to culture.

However, prophetic or revealed knowledge contains the fundamental laws upon which creation is based. These principles never change and are not subject to time or place, as is the case with factual knowledge. Prophetic knowledge is primal and absolute. It is, therefore, of the greatest value. When all outside information and facts are sorted out using the yardstick of this knowledge, reliable and desirable outcomes will ensue. Growth and increase in this knowledge is real enrichment, whereas the growth and increase in information and facts without this network of unchangeable knowledge is of little value and can be confusing. We understand this revealed knowledge once we have been exposed to it because we all share that higher consciousness.

The eternal greed of man is an example of revealed knowledge. A man may first desire (be greedy for) wealth, then security, then love, and finally knowledge. Greed will always exist but the direction and hierarchy of the greed will change.

Fear is another integral part of man's nature. At the lowest level he is afraid of hunger, of animals, of the elements. He may then become afraid of not being loved or of not being acknowledged. Even the Prophets have feared that they may become cut off from revealed knowledge.

Individual knowledge, which is based on the facts that we acquire, is concerned with our circumstantial situation. Revealed knowledge, transmitted by the Prophets, tells us the purpose of our creation and gives us a clear direction through which we may evolve spiritually. We may indeed stumble across some of the revealed knowledge but it will only be by trial and error unless we learn from the selected messengers of these eternal truths, the Prophets.

It is through human knowledge that we acquire technological or scientific knowledge, which have far more to do with the physical realities. Unless made subservient to revealed knowledge, these acquired technologies can also be our doom. However, if they are taken as secondary and subservient to the Prophetic knowledge, they can assist man in his journey towards self-knowledge. Modern technology is only valuable if it enables us to have more time for reflection and study, but generally in today's material society it merely becomes an end in itself.

So the physical knowledge we have gathered will not necessarily help us to enhance our spiritual knowledge. Scientific and technological knowledge is generally material and to do with the physical world, while revealed knowledge relates to totality; its emphasis is more on the inward, the spiritual and the lasting. Man will never be satisfied unless the material is made subservient to the spiritual.

Both types of knowledge have their own specific courtesies. A selfish, acquisitive person can pursue scientific knowledge with success because it does not require the constant self-purification necessary for the seeker of spiritual knowledge. The spiritual seeker progresses along the path of inner knowledge to unlock and reach closer to the source of inner knowledge interacting within him; in this search he becomes the laboratory, the mosque or the monastery, whereas the seeker of outer technology is separate from his laboratory experiments.

The pursuit of material or scientific knowledge tends to enhance individualism and the ego. Generally the scientist becomes the centre of his universe in the discovery and manipulation of these laws; while the cosmic universality of spiritual knowledge demands that the seeker surrenders into it. Indeed the meaning of Islam is 'to surrender'. Once that happens there is a resonance that reverberates within him, echoing the infinite, indescribable song of totality, and reminding him that man is created in order to discover the generosity of his Creator and see His infinite mercy in every situation. If this knowledge is not reflected in his actions and in his thoughts, he does not resonate. Indeed the degree of a man's inner knowledge is reflected in his face and in all his deeds. Inner knowledge is transformative, while mechanistic knowledge can only be measured in terms of prizes and publications. The former lies within the person, the latter outside of him.

The key term to describe revealed knowledge is resonance. Acquired knowledge is entirely intellectual so it functions at a much lower level. However, when a scientist is at the point of making a great discovery or breakthrough, he comes close to the edge of spiritual knowledge as he steps towards the ocean of the unknown. This is why a great scientist like Einstein could say, at the peak of his career: 'I feel like a child on the shore of the ocean, playing with the pebbles of the ocean of knowledge.' In fact, many of the early scientists were monks, living an ascetic life. Mendel, the founder of modern genetics, is an example of this.

So outer and inner technology are not incompatible. Indeed man begins his journey by seeking outer technology. We are programmed to acquire appropriate clothing, shelter and food, all of which need outer technology, but as we move up the hierarchy of search and fulfilment of needs we reach the point where the priority will be fulfilment by application of inner technology, to which outer technology will be subservient and useful.

It is like the usefulnessness of a warm shelter in order to enhance inner qualities of peace and contentment. Indeed we are programmed to desire an outer condition so tranquil and balanced that we can forget about it; we want health and equilibrium in our body so that we transcend body consciousness. Yet, we tend to ignore our bodies and health until we are conscious of an imbalance. Thus outer technology is a first step towards inner technology.

The Law of Opposites

The original Adamic creation began in a tranquil garden, where there was no agitation. In the Garden all desires were fulfilled. However, there was no awareness of the distinction between good and bad. God wanted to reveal the fundamental issue of the opposites on which existence is based; for everything in life is experienced in a duality that is constantly moving from increase to decrease, strength to weakness, happiness to sadness, life to death, to give a few examples. So we are placed on earth in order to experience these opposites; yet in every situation that faces us we naturally veer towards one direction and avoid the other.

All of our behaviour patterns are based on this push-pull mechanism by which we all of us, according to our circumstances or the state of our body and intellect, will wish to interact with that which causes equilibrium and thereby contentment, and repel what causes disequilibrium and thereby discontentment. This mechanism exists on both the physical and mental levels. We love comfort and praise but dislike unpleasant conditions and criticism.

Man, like all other creations, contains within himself the vegetative self, which is concerned with sustenance, growth and reproduction. He also contains the animal self, with its added dimensions of mobility and the ability to react. Man is distinguished from the animal self by his faculty of reasoning and intellect, from which emanates that deeper guideline we call conscience. Thus man constantly seeks that which is conducive to his state of well-being and equilibrium and avoids destruction, confusion and uncertainty.

His natural preference is to want desirable attributes, such as security and longevity. Man, having been created and conceived in the Garden and then seeing its opposite of hell and suffering, will spent the rest of his life striving to return to the state of the Garden — ie, tranquillity, reliability and continuous bliss.

As we grow in awareness we begin to recognize the existence of the opposites within us. On the one hand we have indulgence; on the other we have a complete absence of desire. If these two extremes are balanced, we will end up with self-restraint and modesty. We can be insolent and we can be self-effacing and shy. The balance between these two characteristics is modesty. Another virtue, steadfastness, is between over-excitement and indifference. Self-control lies between rigidity and lack of restraint. Piety is the balance between excessive asceticism and hedonism. These virtues stem from the power of attraction which with the power of repulsion make up the two opposing motivational factors that dictate man's behaviour patterns.

The power of attraction and the power of repulsion are both called bestial power. The power of attraction is connected with the liver and resembles the dog; its centre is the heart. The latter is a savage or predatory type of power and has been symbolised by the pig. This is why they say that the spiritual master rides on his dog and his pig, because these characteristics are within all of us and are our lowest elements. We have to recognize their character if we are to ride on them to safety. The powers of repulsion, for example, ultimately lead us to the high virtues of courage, magnanimity, integrity, composure, fortitude, forbearance, self-containment and endurance.

These virtues are like the centre of a circle; if we are dead in the centre, we possess them — but, if we move to either side, we reach one of the two extremes; eg, courage is half way between recklessness and cowardice. Once these virtues have been acknowledged through wisdom and experience, we have the beginning of the development of the rational self. Wisdom is the highest attribute of the rational self. It is the reservoir of self-knowledge, which is based on the experience of controlling the laws of Reality, which are sub-genetically within us, and which never change. It is wisdom with its associated virtues of intelligence, rationality, clarity of thought and quickness of understanding that will lead us towards the knowledge of justice.

These moral values of goodness, generosity and wisdom have always been accepted in every culture and society. The same values have been acknowledged throughout the history of mankind, but the definition of these values — ie, the way in which they are expressed — differs.

Justice

The question of justice and goodness are inseparable because justice implies good judgement; it is based on the value of goodness and goodness is subject to time. From the point of view of timelessness there is an absolute justice which never changes. However, *in* time there is both absolute justice and relative justice, absolute goodness and relative goodness. It is good to tell the truth but sometimes a truth misplaced can bring about negativity .in relative time. So an event on its own does not determine its goodness or badness, this judgement is time-dependent.

The shorter the time scale that is under consideration, the more injustices are seen. During the course of one day one encounters both good and bad happenings. If one reviews the day within the framework of the week, then the month, and then the year, one will begin to see the justice of all these events. This may not have been apparent during the day itself.

Man's nature is to seek the good and avoid the bad. Hence the nature of Reality must be good because man is not separate from that Reality. So if we experience or judge a situation as being unjust or bad, it is only because of the time frame in which we are looking at it. If we look at man as a creature of time, he will be seen to experience a mixture of good and bad events, the good probably prevailing over the bad. The longer the time frame within which he reviews what has happened to him, the more likely he is to recognize the justice of events. So if man identifies with his body, he will see justice to the extent his objectivity and wisdom allow him. If he identifies with his soul, whatever phenomena take place in the physical and material realms will be understandable as part of the interplay of cause and effect. This awareness itself is the foundation of the recognition of Divine justice.

It is natural that we progress from the material, physical world towards the spiritual and timeless vision. As we increase in experience and in wisdom in the material world, we gain wider understanding that enables us to see the goodness that underlies the perfection of the creational laws, their intricate interplay and their interconnection with the subtler laws. From this pinnacle of increased wisdom, we can look at the horizon of the timeless. At this dimension the question of injustice does not even arise; all is good, all is just.

The physical and material realm is only the kindergarten in which we train and develop our perfection, so that we may reach the edge of the shore of timelessness with its infinite mercy and absolute justice. We are given a licence to play in this kindergarten and imitate absolute justice in preparation for meeting it. Human justice in this world is at best an echo of Divine justice.

The more man's laws are in line with absolute justice, the more lasting are those laws. When man misapplies his freedom in relation to the creational laws that bind him, chaos ensues. Upholding justice is part of the knowledge given to man, of how to apply his freedom to its full capacity within the bounds, through the recognition of those bounds.

There are many *ayat* in the Qur'an enjoining man to justice.

> Surely Allah enjoins the doing of justice and the doing of good (to others)... .
>
> (16:90)

> O, you who believe! Be upright for Allah, bearers of witness with justice, and let not hatred of a people incite you not to act equitably; act equitably, that is nearer to piety, and be careful of (your duty to) Allah; surely Allah is Aware of what you do.
>
> (5:8)

> Surely Allah commands you to make over trusts to their owners and that, when you judge between people, you judge with justice.
>
> (4:58)

> He said: As to him who is unjust, we will chastise him,
> then shall he be returned to his Lord, and He will chastise
> him with an exemplary chastisement.
>
> (18:87)

> And as to those who believe and do good deeds, He will
> pay them fully their rewards; and Allah does not love the
> unjust.
>
> (3:57)

> And Allah sets forth a parable of two men; one of them
> is dumb, not able to do anything, and he is a burden to
> his master; wherever he sends him, he brings no good; can
> he be held equal with him who enjoins what is just, and
> he (himself) is on the right path?
>
> (16:76)

From the above *ayah* we see that justice and the 'path' are
related. Even in existential matters, we all want the smoothest
of journeys. This means we want to be just to ourselves. How
can we do this, if we are not just to the laws of creation?

Reward and Punishment

Everything in nature is benign, for God's bounty is all-encompassing and His mercy is before His anger (wrath). This point is
explained in the following *ayat*:

> On the day that every soul shall find present what it has
> done of good and what it has done of evil, it shall wish
> that between it and that (evil) there were a long duration
> of time; and Allah makes you to be cautious of (retribution
> from) himself; and Allah is Compassionate to the servants.
>
> (3:30)

> Whoever brings a good deed, he shall have ten like it, and
> whoever brings an evil deed, he shall be recompensed only
> with the like of it, and they shall not be dealt with unjustly.
>
> (6:160)

All good deeds will be magnified, while evil actions will only bring about an equal level of retribution, because everything in creation is in expansion.

Both reward and punishment are necessary for they are the fruits or follow-up of all actions that emanate from us. They are not initiated from outside us.

All aspects of disobedience and transgression are incongruities or breaks in a system. The system behind this existence is one of unification; hence all these experiences are non-unifying.

> What! when a misfortune befell you, and you had certainly afflicted (the unbelievers) with twice as much, you begin to say: Whence is this? Say: It is from yourselves; surely Allah has power over all things.
>
> (3:165)

Punishment is the reaction that is applicable only to the slave. It does not contra-indicate the existence of the prior mercy of God. We are judged to be obedient or disobedient after we have acted. The function of punishment is to prevent us from continuing to be disruptive. When spiritual seekers refer to punishment in the context of purification, emptying or polishing, they mean it is a way through which we can wash off the filth and incongruities of disharmony and disobedience.

There is often misunderstanding about the question of those who appear pre-destined to misery and difficulties. One *hadith* that is frequently misinterpreted is this one:

> 'He who is miserable is miserable from his mother's womb.'

One of the meanings of this *hadith* is that the physical traits of the person are determined genetically, so they have already been decided when the foetus is formed. The *hadith* also refers to the knowledge of all events that exist in non-time. However, the person himself, existing in time, has to strive within the limitations of his situation. God's knowledge of the decree does

107

not preclude man's freedom to act, for His knowledge and man's freedom to choose are two different zones and are not related. So it is incumbent upon all of us, whatever our circumstances, to beseech God for His assistance.

Although genetic limitations exert considerable influence on the character, a great deal of change can occur in the person through spiritual development. Indeed some true believers can rise spiritually to such heights that their physical or other disabilities pale into insignificance against their acquired states.

There is no Rule without an Exception

All phenomena that are measurable or experiencable in the sensory world are subject to the law of opposites. Their existence is dependent upon this polarity. If there was only light, we would be unable to distinguish it, and it would be taken for granted. If an awareness of death was not within us, we would not be aware of life, nor could we appreciate it.

In a subtle way within every rule we also notice an inherent opposite or an exception. An example of this is the law of gravity, which prevails in our physical world, but at the boundary of that world the power of gravity ceases. On average the life span of a human being is seventy years. However, there are exceptions who die when over a hundred. Sometimes these exceptions are called miracles but this is only a name to describe logical phenomena, which are exceptions to the general rule.

If there is a river and the average speed of its flow is ten miles an hour, any floating object — if there is no wind or other obstacle to impede it — will travel at ten miles an hour. At the very edge of the river, the object will not move at all. There the molecules of water are almost immobile. At the point where the edge of the water touches the river bank, there is no motion. So the rule is that the average speed of the river's flow is ten miles an hour. The exception is that there is also a molecular layer of water that is motionless, yet it is part of the water in the river.

So within the norm or the rule, there is an exception. The

majority of phenomena follow a norm but there will always be a small part that exhibits abnormal behaviour. This behaviour is absolutely at the edge of the system and, if we take it to its ultimate cutting edge, it becomes the interspace between motion and immobility. Therefore, it no longer exhibits the norm, which applies to the mainstream. This overlap of systems occurs across the board.

Our thinking rational behaviour and indeed the whole foundation of logic and science is based on the phenomenon of cause and effect, and the law of opposites and duality. We exist and develop utilizing this rational foundation with its security, yet exceptions to it exist. Madness is the exception to sanity, as enlightenment is to ordinary consciousness; the former is beyond the laws of causality, as it has to do with the sphere of unification. All intellectual pursuits are based on the balance between the opposites, for this is the general rule in the physical experiential world. The exception to the rule, which encompasses all that, is based on a unitive spectrum.

Reality is based on the rule of time and space; exceptional reality is beyond time and space. Man functions and is familiar with the existential reality but beyond this lies the exceptional reality of infinite time and space. The seeker of truth progresses along the path of rational behaviour up to a point where all processes of cognizance and awareness cease; at that edge subjectively the pure experience of beingness sets in. The rule is being something or another; the exception is pure being. This is the purpose of creation.

Miracles

A miracle can be defined as a break in our comprehension of cause and effect. By necessity, knowledge is limited. If it were not limited, there would be no comprehension. There can be no knowledge unless there are limitations to what we can know. Therefore, whatever is called knowledge intrinsically has bounds. It is like a child whose knowledge is so limited that he cannot catch the sleight of hand, and he considers a magician's trick a miracle. By the same token, anything that we observe in nature, which appears to be incomprehensible or out of the 'norm', is considered by us to be miraculous.

A miracle can also be defined as an interface between the seen and the unseen, the known and unknown. Everything in life has a spectrum — a gross and subtler aspect, a black and a white. Light, for example, at one extreme exhibits its characteristics very much as a wave. At the other extreme, it exhibits itself as a particle. Concerning its behaviour as a particle, it reaches a certain point which is called the Uncertainty Principle of Heisenberg. There are zones in which our knowledge can no longer rely on causality and logic. It is at these zones and beyond that we describe events as miraculous.

This is the farthest point to which we can go in the ocean of this system of knowledge. However, there is another system, another outlook, that knows exactly how that randomness will behave. These two systems are interconnected, and where they overlap, events may occur which the superstitious man sees as miraculous.

In the Qur'an and in our Islamic traditions, there are many references which indicate that man is inherently programmed to know. In fact, the pursuit of science and man's desire for knowledge are an intrinsic proof that there is no such thing as the supernatural. If this is not the case, how is it that man from time immemorial pursues knowledge of the universe around him, by seeking the natural and avoiding or changing the unnatural. Science, thus, must have within it the key to all knowledge.

In a well-known tradition, God, be He exalted, says: "I was a hidden treasure and I wished to be known. Therefore I created creation in order that I might be known." Everything in existence can be known, for all creational reality is based on natural laws, which can be explained by causality. These laws of nature are cosmic, not chaotic. Thus from the viewpoint of all-encompassing (seen and unseen) knowledge, there are no such things as miracles; they exist only within the bounds of our limited comprehension.

110

The ordinary man in his ignorance sees something out of the 'norm' as being a miracle, whereas the men of knowledge see everything as being in the 'norm'. The latter view all creation in its majestic splendour, knowing that the One Who holds it all together is not visible, yet He is in complete control. This is the ultimate magic.

The small aberrations that may intrigue us are of no concern to the men of knowledge. These men are concerned with the flow of the stream, the way it moves, the direction in which it is going, and its Source, not the edges or exceptions which fascinate us, because we often do not see what is closest to us.

Kismet (*Qismah*) — Luck, Fortune

The root of *qismah* (or kismet as it is commonly spelt in English) is *qasama* which means *to share, to apportion, to divide, to distribute, to arrange, to assign*. *Qasim* is the *divider*, and kismet is the outcome of the division or distribution.

Kismet is generally used in the sense of luck or fortune. These meanings relate to success and the achievement of a clearly defined objective. If an objective is to be reached, we need a definition of the resources which will be required to attain that target along a period of time. Our efforts will take place against an environment, where outside factors will constantly impinge, sometimes easing the situation, sometimes creating a reverse effect.

If the target, for example, is to build a house, and the weather is favourable, then less resources and time will be needed. However, if the weather is bad, more resources and time may be required to protect the material and the workers. This example is easy to understand. However, in a complex world, the conflicting factors, including unknown and unforeseeable forces that will impact upon each other, may make it impossible to gauge the outcome.

We express our inadequate knowledge of the model by the terms 'good luck', 'bad luck', 'good fortune' and 'misfortune'.

All these terms imply is a value judgement that those conditions that are favourable to our objective constitute good luck, whilst those that are unfavourable are seen as bad luck.

If we were more knowledgeable we would have a clearer picture of the relevant causes and their effects. A child who discovers a sweet in his pocket considers himself lucky. The mother who has placed the sweet there finds his discovery very straightforward, with no element of surprise or mystique.

Luck is when a desired outcome has been enhanced by an unexpected or one-off occurrence. We usually call an event a misfortune when we expected a desirable outcome, the unusual occurred and the result disappointed us.

Thus the term 'good fortune' or 'luck' can be seen as an expression of ignorance made fortuitously when what we consider desirable or important for our contentment and satisfaction has been met under complex circumstances, which we do not fully comprehend.

Supplication and Prayer

Supplication is a proof of our freedom to act. It is an expression of our objectives, desires or needs. We supplicate at a physical level to regain our health, at a mental level to have a steady mind, at a spiritual level to have a pure heart and be freed from self-inflicted burdens. In this expression lies the first step towards success. The fact that we have expressed that need, whether it is real or not, low or high, is the first step either towards fulfilling or abandoning it.

When we express a desire in prayer, our inner intention as well as our outer behaviour is unified towards that end, so our desire is more likely to be granted. At all levels supplication purifies because a desire or a need is a cause of continuous imbalance, and supplication strives to correct that imbalance. It is like picking up a telescope, because it helps us to focus on our objectives by unifying our needs with a possible way of fulfilling them. On the physical level we move towards our goal, on the mental level we continually concentrate on how we can fulfill our needs, and on the spiritual level we will be guided by the unseen.

People of spiritual insight know that the true desire will always be fulfilled. If a child, for example, genuinely desires a permissible object and asks for it persistently, he will eventually obtain it. It is the same with supplication. Reality will ultimately provide the remedy that will rebalance one. At first supplication may be superficial but the more persistent and serious it is, and the more it stems from one's inner depths, the more one is likely to receive it.

The meaning of supplication at a human level is thus a clarification and an awareness of needs and desires. It is hoped at the unseen level that the expression of these objectives will bring about the right elements that are required for their fulfilment.

Causality and Repentance

Gross outer events can sometimes lead to a subtle reaction. If over a period of time, for example, one does not take care of the condition of the tyres on the car, they will eventually give out. One has set up a chain of events, a channel, which will finally lead to that inevitable catastrophe. It is possible, however, through the interlinks between these systems of the gross and the subtle, the outcome of that hypothetical chain will result in the form of a dream, in which a car accident takes place. It is decreed that a certain outcome will occur as a result of one's actions but that outcome may be transferred to a subtler realm. Thus, physical actions can result in happenings that are subtle and vice versa.

We cannot speak about decree and destiny in their totality without considering all the systems that are at play in the visible and invisible, in matter and energy. Therefore, the decree, which is absolute, and in one sense unchangeable because it is based on causality, can still have an unexpected outcome although this outcome would be a mirror image in the subtle sense of the physical/material system.

The reverse of this is also true. A sudden inspiration that gives us a vision of fame and fortune in a far-off land can result in a physical reality. In the total system, there is no barrier between the gross and the subtle.

There are many teachings in our traditions which reflect this. We have, for example, the case of the Prophet Nuh, to whom we have previously referred. When he came to his people, they had already committed so much erroneous and disturbing action that it was not only affecting their lives but also changing their entire environment. Through his prophetic insight, Nuh could see that his people's actions had caused so much ecological disturbance that he foresaw the deluge coming. He implored them to repent and change their ways, in the hope that the flood could be averted or diminished. They would not change, and Nuh realized that it was too late for repentance; destiny in the form of the floods was inevitable.

There are many traditions that say a time will come when our supplications will not be accepted. God, be He Exalted, says in the Holy Qur'an:

> ...and do not speak to Me in respect of those who are unjust; surely they shall be drowned.
>
> (23:27)

This means that there are limits to every situation and there will be cases when the decree cannot be changed.

If, for example, we catch a case of cancer in its early stages, we may be able, through diet, healthier living and appropriate remedies to prevent the cancer-producing cells from increasing. If this does not happen early on in the sickness, we may have to resort to surgery or chemotherapy; and eventually a time will come, when nothing will be able to arrest the progress of the disease.

Any chain of events will eventually reach a stage where intercession is ineffective. The knowledge of these stages is beyond our comprehension. This is why we say this knowledge only exists with God. However, aspects of it may be revealed to us in specific situations.

In the Qur'an and traditions there are many descriptions of situations where it is necessary to completely abandon a system. This was the case with the Prophet Nuh when he realized it was too late to alter the course of destiny. He constructed his ark and sailed away on the flood to safety.

This is the meaning of repentance, of asking to be saved from the outcome of our past ignorant actions. If we have genuinely acted in ignorance, we will be saved anyway, because inherently we do not know what is happening. This is why we say: 'Our actions are as good as our intentions', or 'as good as the direction we are taking'.

If we set out on the path of the discovery of Reality, through the knowledge of its laws and their application, then we will come to know these rules according to the extent of the openness and purity of our hearts. The pure heart is the ultimate receiver of that knowledge.

The Search for Happiness

The development of the faculty of reasoning begins from childhood. This process of growth and cognizance starts from the child's assessment of his immediate environment, progressing as he grows to maturity in the mental and intellectual realms. The adult attempts to achieve harmony and equilibrium at all levels, be it the physical harmony of a balanced room temperature or intellectual or spiritual harmony.

A person with a certain measure of intelligence may realize that the particular environment he is in is not conducive to his physical health or material well-being. Hence he reaches the conclusion that migration is necessary. Animals do this naturally; man reaches this conclusion through a process of reasoning, counselling and investigation.

The search for equilibrium begins with the physical and ends up in most natural cases with concern for inner spiritual development. So when the person begins with a great deal of concern about his physical harmony and well-being, he often ends with the reverse situation — ie, greater concern about his inner state. This is a natural progression because his physical activity is at its maximum at the beginning of his life. He begins with maximum physical activity, minimum inner. If the situation is not reversed as he grows older, you have the pitiful sight of the old man trying to act as a young boy. This is often the fate of old people in societies that have not evolved spiritually.

It is an infallible law of Reality that we are programmed in every situation and at every level sub-genetically to seek equilibrium. Contentment with God is the recognition of this firmly ingrained law. Each tribe, society, nation or culture is ultimately seeking equilibrium within their specific environment, although each individual search will manifest a different flavour.

The ultimate definition of betterment at the physical level — ie, bodily comfort, material security, companionship — means to be least disturbed for the maximum time. In other words, peace and satisfaction are achieved by attaining what is conducive for the longest period of time or avoiding that which is not conducive. Happiness is inversely proportionate to demands and expectations; the less the demands and expectations, the higher the level of contentment and equilibrium.

Human beings continuously strive for outer betterment as represented by material possessions but tend to neglect the search for inner betterment. So many people today end their lives surrounded by every material luxury yet disappointed and embittered, dependent on either alcohol or tranquillizers. Man's continuous desire for peace and contentment is a trial run of preparation for the next phase of existence, which is in infinite time after death. If he cannot find these states in a more natural way, he may resort to artificial inducements. When even these props fail him, he may try to take his life. Suicides are only confirming the unfulfilled purposelessness of their lives.

Throughout history we find mankind demanding equality Indeed, most of our present political and economic systems, be they democratic or otherwise, uphold this ideal, although very little thought is given to its real meaning.

We all desire the material comforts we see others possess; yet it is inconceivable that everybody will have an identical possibility of acquisition and subsequent benefit from these belongings. The writer's interpretation is that it is not so much the actual material possessions that we seek but the effect and outcome of their acquisition upon the acquirer. It is not the metal and rubber of the sports car that we love; it is the image of happiness and pleasure on the face of the proud owner that we long for, in addition to whatever utility value the article may have.

We all know that there is no end to material pleasure. We can conclude purely from the result of an arithmetical exercise that it would be impossible for us to collect, store and use all conceivable material objects which we may desire from time to time. At the same time we have this urge towards equality. What we are really demanding is the access to or possibility of that state of contentment, satisfaction and freedom from want, which the acquisition of these goods brings. Our goal, therefore, is freedom and equilibrium. We are seeking the opportunity to exercise the ultimate objective of being physically, mentally and intellectually in a state of equilibrium free of agitation and anxieties.

Reality in itself, provides that equal opportunity but man imposes his own restrictions through his greed and other weaknesses. His abuse of the superficial barriers of colour, creed, nationality and other artificial factors creates a materialistic menace with the 'haves' and 'have nots' at each other's throats.

Man forgets that material objects only make a limited contribution to his total inner and outer happiness. The outer needs that give him physical well-being are only necessary if they assist his inner awakening, without which no amount of material acquisition suffices. The frequently heard cries of inequality thus arise from our misunderstanding and ignorance. What we are really seeking is equity. This can be defined as equal opportunity and potential, without a built-in bias or favouritism to categorize and influence, that is not based on rationally acceptable justifications such as performance, ability, education etc. Everyone knows that no two fingers are the same, let alone two people, yet we expect everyone to have the same potential.

It is interesting to note that mankind's primal demand for equity is based on the fact that we all intrinsically have the same opportunity and personal freedom to achieve spiritual awakening to its ultimate limitations. We know that God is just but man's justice is only relative. Hence we expect equity because it is godly, but equality is to do with the world and man, so we know it can never be absolute.

Why People Differ

People differ in their capacity for good and evil. The inner lower tendencies differ according to their subtlety and strength. This is what is referred to as the degree of closeness or furtherance from God.

If we imagine the world to be a giant cooking pot in which we are all being cooked at varying speeds, according to our individual states, we will discover that each one of us is given certain limitations, freedoms and possibilities for action suitable to our specific situation. A king has a country at his command, while a blind man, without legs, has as his horizon a circle with a two foot radius around him. Ultimately, if they progress spiritually, they will make the same discovery. The king will find out that nothing in this world will satisfy him and that true satisfaction can only come from inner knowledge, as will the blind man.

While we may differ as to varying capacities on the micro level, we do not differ in our potential for reaching the same point of inner contentment and realization. Each one of us is the project of the Creator, and the objective of that project is the discovery of the infallibility of the Creator and the perfection of His laws.

So our differences only exist for us to discover our non-difference. The differences between men are superficial although, to the child or those who are less developed spiritually, the distinctions of race, colour, creed, physical and intellectual types may seem enormous. The man of wisdom, however, goes to the essence; for him each star has its spectrum of vibration but a star is always a star. Ultimately, each one of us exudes the same thing. We all have positive and negative elements within us. The outer differences of language or colour are diversities based upon a foundation of similarity. Cultural differences are merely the outer habits to which society is accustomed. The basic motive and original cause of these habits is similar in all cultures and societies.

We all come from the same Source, are sustained by the same Source, and at the end collapse back again into that Source. The question we must ask is about the extent of our submission to the circumstances in which we find ourselves.

The following tradition is related from the Blessed Prophet:

'People are like gold and silver mines. The good of them before Islam is the same as the good of them in Islam.'[50]

Islam is only the process of purification by which the good is extracted from the debris. It is not going to affect the metal content. This is already done, based on other factors, such as genes and environment. Islam is simply a more efficient method in that it enables man to achieve his objective and fulfill his purpose of life more quickly.

People, like mines, contain a lot of debris as well as sudden seams of pure gold. Hence it is up to us to struggle to dispose of the rubbish within us, and develop the science and technology of inner meaning — ie, inner development and purification.

In the *Fusus al-Hikam* (Seals of Wisdom) in the chapter of ' The Seal of the Wisdom of being lost in love in the word of Ibrahim', Muhyi al-Din ibn 'Arabi says:

'That which was in your fixed reality appears in your manifestations and what Truth has done has only caused a fragrance of existence upon you. So do not praise yourself, and do not condemn except yourself, for there is nothing left upon you of Truth (Reality) except praise for that existence that belongs to Him and not to us.'[51]

Imam 'Ali ibn Abi Talib relates the following Prophetic *hadith* in *Nahj al-Balaghah*:

'He who finds goodness let him praise Allah, and whoever
sees and finds other than that let him only blame himself.'

God guides whom He wishes. We do not guide whom we love.
If we wish somebody to be guided, he too has to desire it, behave
properly, and become at one with God's decree; for God has
given the freedom to that individual to remain at a loss or to
reconnect with what he is already connected to without his knowledge. Man has been given the freedom to flounder or swim.
God's wish is according to God's laws. His law includes the
freedom of the individual, whether he wants to acknowledge it
or not. The individual himself must decide he wants to see the
light in this tunnel of life. We cannot impose this wish on others.
God has given the capacity of discrimination to everybody and
made it easy for us to see. However, the majority do not comprehend, and those of us who do are powerless to guide those
whom we love, for it is God's law that has to be followed in
order for that awakening to occur.

Selective Search

Throughout the ages people who seek spiritual guidance, whether
because of their limited knowledge or the dictates of expediency,
often take part of the meaning of a story rather than the whole,
thus misleading themselves and others.

> Woe, then, to those who write the book with their hands
> and then say: This is from Allah, so that they may take
> for it a small price; therefore woe to them for what their
> hands have written and woe to them for what they earn.
>
> (2:79)

There is always the danger of the selective *nafs* choosing what
it likes and disregarding what is not conducive. The Qur'an
places the responsibility squarely upon the individual.

Yea! whoever earns evil and his sins beset him on every
side, these are the inmates of the fire; in it they shall abide.

(2:81)

Reality is multi-dimensional; we cannot take parts of it and
neglect other aspects as may suit our emotions. It is one totally
integrated, interwoven model.

Bone of Contention

The following Qur'anic *ayat* are among those relevant to the
question of whether man is compelled by God to wrong action
or has been given free will, which have been both deliberately
or inadvertently misinterpreted.

...but He causes to err whom He pleases and guides whom
He pleases; and most certainly you will be questioned as
to what you did.

(16:93)

Surely you cannot guide whom you love, but Allah guides
whom He pleases, and He knows best the followers of the
right way.

(28:56)

Both these *ayat* are often quoted by those who claim that
everything is in God's hands and nothing in man's. The correct
interpretation is that the ultimate capability is in God's hands
as everything in creation emanates from this one Source. If God
through His power of awakening had caused all His creation to
be knowing, there would have been no differentiation between
good and bad, and no meaning of punishment or reward. All
knowledge is ultimately from God and He has created in man
the ability to perceive. If He had forced him to be the owner of
that guidance, he would not have known the meaning of being
at a loss. His programme is that of participative evolution. The
individual will come to realize the unifying Cause from Which
he arose, by means of Which he was sustained and developed

121

and to Which he has returned after recognition of the worldly existence (duality), which is based all along on a unified all-encompassing timeless Reality.

God only selects to the extent that man elects to understand God's laws and follow them. God selects a successful farmer in the sense that the farmer chooses to observe the natural laws of growth and harvest and applies his skills in line with these natural laws. If he does this the farmer has elected himself to be successful, but if he falls a prey to ignorance he will be punished by failure because he will have neglected the laws of his Creator.

The Creator and Created

The relationship of the world to its Creator is not like that of the house to the builder, nor like that of the writer to his writing. These situations are independent of their instigator in the sense that the physical act of writing stops when the writer completes his work, but what has previously been created — ie, the house or the book — remains.

The relationship is similar to that between speech and the speaker. Once the speaker ceases to speak, his speech disappears. Equally it resembles the light of the sun in the darkness of space. The existence of the sun continues because it has its own existence. In the same way, speaking is not a part of the speaker but it is his action and his doing; the light that can be seen in space is not a part of the sun but an overflow from it; so this creational world is not part of the Creator but it is a grace or an effulgence that emanates from him.

All life emanates from the sun and without it there would have been no creation. However, the sun alone does not cast a shadow; it is 'I' who cast the shadow. It is true to say that the shadow is caused by the sun, but equally the shadow is caused by me, through my interaction with the sun. Without the sun there would be no me, hence no shadow. However, the choice of casting the shadow rests in my hands. Bad action, like the shadow, is not from the sun; it springs from my abuse or ignorance.

There is an admixture between my will and the permanent Divine will or the will of the sun. This situation sometimes gives rise to confusion. The Absolute will is from the Divine Creator, but I decide whether or not to cast a shadow; so the essence of all this is created by God but the specificity of it is made by me, because there is a personal will. Ultimately there is no power except God's but to me has been delegated limited freedom of action.

A Better Destiny

Man is programmed to be constantly striving for a better life for himself through the knowledge of the decree. This striving is part of man's destiny.

Mawlana Jalal al-Din al-Rumi said:

> 'Leaving ignorance teaches me that you can escape from one destiny to another, but this is not against destiny because striving is part of destiny.'

Here decree and destiny are equated: man's inherent tendency is to strive, develop and improve, because striving at all times is in his destiny.

Imam 'Ali ibn Abi Talib, when he fled from under a crumbling wall, explained in an earlier quoted *hadith*, that he had escaped destiny by the decree. It had been decreed that he would see the wall was beginning to crumble and he was given enough time to flee before the wall collapsed. So on this occasion it was the decree of God that the Imam should be saved, and the Imam simply followed God's will.

From the Commentary of Ibn Abi'l-Hadid expounding upon *Nahj al-Balaghah* of Imam 'Ali ibn Abi Talib, Khutbah No. 132, we have an incident related concerning 'Umar ibn al-Khattab during one of his journeys to Syria. Before entering the country, 'Umar was told that it was stricken with plague. He assembled his people and asked them what he should do. They unanimously said he should not enter the country, except for

Abu 'Ubaydah ibn al-Jar who was the leader of the Muslim forces in Syria. He objected to 'Umar not going in to the town, saying:

> 'O Commander of the Faithful, are you running from the decree of Allah?'

'Umar answered:

> 'Yes, I run from the decree of Allah, by the decree of Allah, to the decree of Allah. I do not want to die. I want to worship the Everlasting Who is in me, for as long as I am able. I do the best I can until the Everlasting takes hold of what has been entrusted into my custody, which is my life. Whilst it is in my hands, I have to do the best by it.'

When the Blessed Prophet was asked:

> 'Are we in a situation that the affair has been completed (in an affair that is finished with) or in an affair that is being reviewed?'

The Blessed Prophet answered:

> 'We are in an affair that has been completed and we are in an affair that is being reviewed and revised constantly.'

This means that while the laws that govern this existence are fixed, what is not finished, and what is subject to review, is our attempt at unifying what is given to us as apparent freedom with the non-freedom of the moment. Once we realize that there are certain factors in nature that cannot change, we can begin to change ourselves.

> 'And you shall not find any change in the *Sunnah* of God.'

The fact that creation has been made for evolution cannot be changed; what can be revised and changed is the extent of our own spiritual evolvement. God's knowledge of our ultimate destiny in no way impinges on our freedom to choose, and does not absolve us from the responsibility to act.

124

> And when We wish to destroy a town, We send Our commandment to the people of it who lead easy lives, but they transgress therein; thus the word proves true against it, so We destroy it with utter destruction.
>
> (17:16)

Nothing in creation happens without a cause. Amongst the important causes of the destruction of a culture is excess. This brings about decadence and final collapse. So it is man who brings about his own doom through his ignorant actions. The angelic powers are simply the programmed energies that carry out that finality.

> Allah has promised to those of you who believe and do good that He will most certainly make them rulers in the earth as He made rulers those before them, and that He will most certainly establish for them their religion which He has chosen for them, and that He will most certainly, after their fear, give them security in exchange; they shall serve Me, not associating aught with Me; and whoever is ungrateful after this, these it is who are the transgressors.
>
> (24:55)

The religion (*din*) of God is abandonment unto God, which is the religion of Islam (*din al-Islam*).

The Free Man

We have hoped to share with the reader the knowledge that there are situations which are determined and which we cannot change, yet within any determined situation there are areas of apparent freedom.

The fact that we will all die eventually, and that the sun and moon move in prescribed orbits, are but examples of determined conditions, the outcomes of which we can predict with certainty. We can calculate, for example, the exact time of an eclipse. As for the areas of freedom, these are the opportunities we have to

125

move about and experiment with so that we may delineate the bounds; the bounds being that the more we act without any expectation, the greater the freedom of our action. We call it 'free action' when we act 'for the sake of God', or acting for 'its own sake', without any expectations of any reward. When this happens reward is more likely to come to us spontaneously and we will not suffer from the consequences of our attachments.

The so-called 'free man' or the 'man of God' is only acting in harmony with the laws of creation. Freedom implies harmony; even if the person is in a state of outer struggle, this is only due to his attempt to unify a situation that appears to be without unity.

He acts diligently, forcefully and single-mindedly, yet there is nothing of his personality in his actions because there is no self. This is the road to freedom. The 'man of God' has tested the hypothesis that God's mercy is all-encompassing, in every situation and at all times. He recognizes that the boundaries are the keys to the recognition of the free will of God. Thus, he frees his own will, and the free will of God prevails. The will of God is timeless. The 'man of God' is biologically subject to time, but his actions are based on values that are beyond the constrictions of time.

The title of 'free man' is misleading for a man can only be a bondsman of the absolute Reality. This title is therefore a contradiction in terms. He can only exert his capacity to the maximum without any expectations at any given moment. He is living in the 'now', not acting on an impulse of yesterday, or the whim of tomorrow. Yesterday has made its impact on him — its imprint remains — and tomorrow's plans lie before him, but his 'now' is full. At the moment of action, his concentration is complete, for he acts as though nothing else existed, with full power and awareness and with no expectations of personal rewards. The real reward will come from his witnessing of the unfolding for others; for there is no otherness anyway, there is only the unfolding of Reality.

The man of God is like a stone on the riverbed witnessing

what moves above and around him. He witnesses destiny yet his inner core is secure. He is like a willow tree; the branches and leaves follow the wind of destiny, while the roots are firmly buried in the ground. His inner certainty is unshakable whereas his outer circumstances are in constant change, his inwardness forever secure, his outwardness in a state of flux. He acts in this world in a completely dedicated yet connected way. If his connection is total, so too is his disconnection. He is in this world but does not belong to it. It is not that he is separate from the world; rather, he lives each moment with the freedom and clarity that can only be brought about by the state of complete surrender that is true Islam.

He may be subjected to afflictions but these are the afflictions of the 'free man'. Many of the Prophets subjected themselves to such afflictions. They could have left their people or forced them to behave correctly but they were all men who were there to unveil for their people the truth of this existence. They are there to shed light from their purer mirrors into dustier mirrors, for people to be able to clean their own mirrors and act as agents for their inner development and awakening.

Men of knowledge often know their eventual destiny in this life. This was the case with Imam Husayn. However, he cannot be blamed because he did not save his life for the constraints were such that a man of his spiritual status and utter connection with truth could not pay allegiance to a drunken despot like Yazid. The state of the 'free man' is that he is not subject to inner or outer blame, because he is completely integrated with the situation around him. Hence he is free in the sense that he will not look back and regret any of his actions. We, on the other hand, may look back at events and wish we had not acted erroneously for we may not have been sufficiently aware of all the factors to make the correct decision, nor were we fully connected and in submission to Reality's laws.

An earlier quoted *hadith* related from Imam Ja'far al-Sadiq summarizes the true state of affairs concerning decree and destiny. It explains that as far as the decree is concerned, people

127

hold to three viewpoints. One alleges that the affair is in man's hands. The second alleges that God forces all His slaves as He wills, and also forces them by what they cannot tolerate. The third viewpoint holds that God has demanded from His slaves what they can do, and does not burden them with what they cannot. This is the viewpoint of the man who knows how to praise God and, if he commits error, to ask forgiveness. This is the true Muslim.

This view falls between the two extremes of those, who on the one hand, say: 'everything is from God, including all of my wrong actions', to the other extreme, 'God has delegated His Power to us so whatever we do is right.' It is both and neither. If a person says that man is completely free, he is speaking the truth from the angle that man has been given freedom of action. Yet when somebody else says that man is completely constricted, he is also correct, in that man's inherent tendency is to seek equilibrium, avoid disharmony and that which he considers undesirable. The full truth is that man is free in the world of constriction. He is forced with choice. Imam al-Ghazzali described him as being 'in a station between the two stations'.

The Imam means by this that man is free in so far as his actions are concerned because his actions are not confirmed, while those of nature are completely programmed. He is forced in as far as his actions are not completely under his control as God's actions are under His. Thus he is able to perform freely in certain circumstances yet remains a creature subject to the overall control of His Creator.

We are bound and we are free. The bonds become clearer as we follow them, and our subtlety increases. Initially there appear to be no bonds, but the more our awareness develops the clearer the limits become, until such time as we cannot move unless our movement is completely connected with our situation.

The spiritual seeker who wishes to achieve this state of freedom has to go through the practices of continuous and spontaneous remembrance and regular stock-taking of his actions and intentions. He should pray to God in gratitude for his good actions so that God may increase him in goodness and save him from arrogance. When he has done wrong he should pray for forgiveness to keep him in a state of proper remembrance. He should pray continuously to God to increase him in spiritual knowledge and strength. The constant review of his intentions ends up with spontaneous correct action. Then he will reach the state of the awakened being, who is so much a slave that he is free of his slavery.

Conclusion

Genuine abandonment, submission and surrender brings about a state of total awareness, connection and purity, which is close to pure consciousness. The self then becomes like a pure mirror reflecting the primal original light of truth — a unific reality without the see-sawing confusion of duality. This state is man's destiny.

We are intended to taste, desire and develop towards achieving this state and remain in its station. This is the worthy destiny for a noble creature. So from this viewpoint there is but one destiny for all, and the backdrops and personal biographies are of little relevance. They are insignificant events compared with the final triumph of returning to the Source from which we came; except now we know the Truth by the light of that Truth itself. Before there was a hint of it, belief in it, and occasional glimpses of realizing it.

Man comes from the unific state of unseen oneness to the creational duality of this life on earth and he returns back via a new consciousness to witness again the infinite Reality from which he springs. This is what is decreed. Whenever it is achieved consciously or by death, man has fulfilled his destiny by the decree. This decree is interactional and participative and therefore the state of the final destiny will be subject to the choice of the individual as he interacts with the original creational intention — to know the Cause behind all, the Creator, to unify and consciously remove the veil of ego and separateness. Thus he arrives where one already was, with the One, God, the Exalted.

Glossary

The following is an expanded glossary of the key Arabic terms used by the author, arranged according to the English alphabet. Transliteration used throughout this book is based on the American Library of Congress system.

Allah	God; literally "the God"; the name that designates the source from which all things seen and unseen emanate. The name Allah encompasses all the Divine Names, such as, *al-Rahman*, the Beneficent, and *al-'Alim*, the Knower (of all things).
'aql	Faculty of reason, intelligence, discernment, rationality, mind, intellect. From the verb *'aqala*: to keep back (a camel by tying its foreleg), to detain, confine, to be restricted, be reasonable, understand, have intelligence, realize. This implies that true reason and intelligence can only be realized by keeping back the lower self (see *nafs*). The plural is *'uqul*.
ayah, ayat	Qur'anic verse; sign or mark.
din	Usually translated to mean religion, the word strongly implies transaction between the Bestower (Allah) and the indebted (man), because the verbal root is *dana*: to owe, be indebted to, take a loan, to be inferior. Hence, living the *din* means repaying one's debt to the Creator, or indeed, behaving as befits the high station of man in creation.
hadith	Tradition, saying (usually of the Blessed Prophet but sometimes related by the Holy Imams, relating his deeds and utterances); speech, account, narrative. From the verb *hadatha*: to

happen, be new; and from *haddatha*: to relate, report, speak about.

haqiqah Truth, fact, reality; the true nature of creation. From the verb *haqqa*: to be true, right, just.

iman Faith, trust, belief. From the verb *amana*: to believe (in). Other words from the same root are *amina*, to be secure, to trust; *amn*, peace, security, protection; *amin* (designation of the Prophet), trustworthy, faithful, loyal, honest; *mu'min*, believing, faithful.

jabarut Omnipotence, power, might, tyranny. The word is derived from *jabara*: to restore, force, compel, set (broken bones), bring back to normal. Sufis use the term to describe the world of divine names and attributes — the middle world between the physical world and the world of the unseen, which is called *malakut*.

kafir, kuffar Denier (of the existence of Allah), one who covers up (the truth), ingrate. From the verb *kafara*: to cover, hide, be ungrateful, not to believe.

kufr Denial, unbelief, ingratitude (see *kafir*).

lata'if Subtleties, witticism, joke, quip, jest. From *latafa*: to be kind and friendly.

malakut Realm, kingdom, empire, sovereignty, kingship, royalty. The word is derived from *malaka*: to take in possession, to take over, to rule. Sufis use the term to describe the world of the unseen, from which emanates the world of the souls and spirits, which through enforced decrees and laws are manifested into the kingdom.

mu'min Believing, faithful; believer (see *iman*).

nafs Self, soul, mind, human being. The *nafs* includes man's innate nature, his genetic predisposition, and his conditioned behaviour. Its manifestation may be base and animalistic, or spiritually elevated, according to the state of its purity. From the verb *nafusa*: to be precious, valuable. It is also related to *naffasa*: to cheer up, reassure, relieve; and *tanaffasa*: to breathe, inhale, pause for a rest.

rizq Livelihood, means of living, subsistence, daily bread, boon, blessing (of God), property, possession, wealth, income, pay, wages, emergency rations. From *razaqa*: to provide with the means of sustenance, to bestow (from God). God the Provider of all is called *al-Razzaq*, the Maintaining Provider.

ruh Spirit, soul. From the verb *raha*: to go away, leave, begin, set out. Derived from this root are *rawwaha*: to refresh, relax, rest; *arwaha*: to release, relieve, soothe; *istarwaha*: to breathe, smell, be refreshed, be calm, happy, glad; *rih*: wind; *Ruhu-llah*: spirit of Allah, a title given to particularly pious and ascetic people such as the prophet Jesus.

shari'ah Revealed Islamic law or code of conduct, outward path. From the verb *shara'a*: to begin, enter, unbind, introduce, prescribe, give (laws). *Shari'* means road or spring. It is the complement and container of *haqiqah*, for the waters that gush from Reality's spring cannot be contained or drunk from except by a proper vessel.

shirk Associating other-than-Allah with Allah, idolatry, polytheism. From the verb *sharika*: to be a companion, to share, participate, associate. A *mushrik* perpetuates this association.

sunnah	Way, habitual custom, line of conduct; used in reference to Allah or the Prophet. From the verb *sanna*: to shape, form, prescribe, enact, establish.
surah	Chapter of the Qur'an, sign, degree or rank. From the verb, *sara*: to mount a wall; or from *sawwara*: to enclose, fence in.
tawhid	Divine unity, union; belief in Allah's oneness. From the verb *wahada*: to be alone, unique, singular, unmatched, without equal. Derivations include *wahhada*: to unite, unify, connect, join, profess belief in the oneness of God; *wahdah*: oneness, singleness, seclusion, self-containment; *al-Wahid*: the One; *al-Ahad*: the Singular without number (attribute of Allah).
ummah	Nation, people; generation, Muhammad's community, the Muslims. From the verb *amma*: to go, betake oneself, lead the way, lead by one's example; to lead in prayer. It refers to a society that believes and lives the Islamic values in their totality and treats this life as a training ground for the hereafter. This society would adhere fully to the tenets of the Qur'an and the teachings of the Blessed Prophet Muhammad.
zakah	Purity; justness, integrity, honesty; justification, vindication; giving alms, charity; alms tax (obligatory under Islamic law.)

Bibliography

The sources for the Sayings of the Blessed Prophet and the Holy Imams quoted in this book are:

— *Kitab al-Tawhid* by Shaykh al-Saduq from an edition published by Dar al Ma'arifa, Lebanon

— *Tuhaf al-'Uqul 'an Al al-Rasul* by Shaykh al-Harrani, from an edition published in Beirut, Lebanon

— *'Ilm al-Yaqin fi Usul al-Din*
by Fayd al-Kashani

— *Al-Kafi* by Muhammad ibn Ya'qub Al-Kulayni

— *Alf Kalimah Mukhtarah*, a collection of Imam 'Ali's Sayings, published in Najaf, Iraq.

Any Qur'anic verses that appear in English have been taken from the translation by M. H. Shakir, published by Tahrike Tarsile Qur'an. Inc., New York, 1982.

Notes

We include the Arabic for the sayings quoted in the book for
those interested. The translations made from the original Arabic
which appear in this book have not been rendered verbatim but
edited slightly for our readers' benefit.

١ ـ إن الله عزّ وجلّ خلق الخلق فعلم ما هم سائرون إليه، وأمرهم
ونهاهم، فما أمرهم به من شيء فقد جعل لهم السبيل إلى الأخذ به ، وما
نهاهم عنه من شيء فقد جعل لهم السبيل إلى تركه، ولا يكونوا آخذين ولا
تاركين إلا بإذن الله.

٢ ـ قال: قال رسول الله: من زعم أن الله تبارك وتعالىٰ يأمر بالسوء
والفحشاء فقد كذب على الله، ومن زعم أن الخير والشر بغير مشيّة الله
فقد أخرج الله من سلطانه ، ومن زعم أن المعاصي بغير قوّة الله فقد
كذب على الله، ومن كذب على الله أدخله الله النار.

٣ ـ كما أن بادي النعم من الله عزّ وجلّ وقد نحلكموه، فكذلك الشر
من أنفسكم وإن جرى به قدره.

٤ ـ سُئل أمير المؤمنين علي (ع) عن القدر فقال: أُقصر أم أطيل؟
قيل: بل تقصر فقال: جلّ الله أن يريد الفحشاء وعن أن يكون في ملكه
ما لا يشاء.

٥ ـ عن أبي جعفر وأبي عبد الله (ع) قالا:
ان الله عزّ وجلّ أرحم بخلقه من أن يجبر خلقه على الذنوب ثم يعذبهم
عليها، والله اعزّ من أن يريد امراً فلا يكون.

٦ ـ إن الناس في القدر على ثلاثة أوجه: رجل يزعم أن الله عزّ وجلّ
أجبر الناس على المعاصي فهذا قد ظلم الله في حكمه فهو كافر، ورجل
يزعم أن الأمر مفوّض إليهم فهذا قد أوهن الله في سلطانه فهو كافر ،

ورجل يزعم أن الله كلّف العباد ما يطيقون ولم يكلّفهم ما لا يطيقون وإذا أحسن حمد الله وإذا أساء استغفر الله فهذا مسلم بالغ.

٧ ـ عن محمد بن عجلان، قال:

قلت لابي عبد الله (ع): فوّض الله الأمر إلى العباد؟ فقال: الله أكرم من أن يفوض إليهم، الله أعدل من أن يجبر عبداً على فعل ثمّ يعذبه عليه.

٨ ـ عن أبي الحسن الرضا عليه السلام، قال: ذكر عنده الجبر والتفويض، فقال: ألا أعطيكم في هذا أصلا لا تختلفون فيه ولا تخاصمون عليه أحدا إلا كسرتموه، قلنا: إن رأيت ذلك، فقال: إن الله عزّ وجلّ لم يطع بإكراه، ولم يعص بغلبة ولم يهمل العباد في ملكه، هو المالك لما ملّكهم، والقادر على ما أقدرهم عليه.

٩ ـ قال: لا جبر ولا تفويض ولكن أمر بين أمرين، قال: قلت: وما أمر بين أمرين؟ قال: مثل ذلك مثل رجل رأيته على معصية فنهيته فلم ينته فتركته ففعل تلك المعصية، فليس حيث لم يقبل منك فتركته أنت الذي أمرته بالمعصية.

١٠ ـ عن أبي الحسن الرضا عليه السلام، قال: سألته فقلت له: الله فوّض الأمر إلى العباد؟ قال: أعزّ من ذلك ، قلت: فأجبرهم على المعاصي؟ قال: الله أعدل وأحكم من ذلك، ثم قال: قال الله عزّ وجلّ: يا ابن آدم أنا اولىٰ بحسناتك منك، وأنت أولى بسيئاتك مني، عملت المعاصي بقوّتي التي جعلتها فيك.

١١ ـ قال أبو عبد الله عليه السلام: أخبرني عمّا اختلف فيه من خلفت من موالينا، قال: قلت: في الجبر والتفويض، قال: فسلني، قلت: أجبر الله العباد على المعاصي؟ قال: الله أقهر لهم من ذلك قال: قلت: ففوّض إليهم؟ قال: الله أقدر عليهم من ذلك، قال: قلت: فأي شيء هذا أصلحك الله؟ قال: فقلب يده مرتين أو ثلاثا، ثم قال: لو أجبتك فيه

137

لكفرت.

١٢ ـ أبي رحمه الله، قال: حدثنا سعد بن عبد الله، قال: حدثنا أحمد بن محمد بن عيسى، عن محمد بن خالد البرقي، عن عبد الملك بن عنترة الشيباني، عن أبيه، عن جده، قال: جاء رجل إلى أمير المؤمنين عليه السلام فقال: يا أمير المؤمنين أخبرني عن القدر، قال عليه السلام: بحر عميق فلا تلجه، قال: يا أمير المؤمنين أخبرني عن القدر، قال عليه السلام: طريق مظلم فلا تسلكه، قال: يا أمير المؤمنين أخبرني عن القدر، قال عليه السلام: سر الله فلا تكلفه قال: يا أمير المؤمنين أخبرني عن القدر، فقال أمير المؤمنين عليه السلام: أما إذا أبيت فإني سائلك، أخبرني أكانت رحمة الله للعباد قبل أعمال العباد أم كانت أعمال العباد قبل رحمة الله؟! قال: فقال له الرجل: بل كانت رحمة الله للعباد قبل أعمال العباد، فقال أمير المؤمنين عليه السلام: قوموا فسلموا على أخيكم فقد أسلم وقد كان كافرا، قال: وانطلق الرجل غير بعيد، ثم انصرف اليه فقال له: يا أمير المؤمنين أبالمشيّة الأولى نقوم ونقعد ونقبض ونبسط؟ فقال له أمير المؤمنين عليه السلام: وإنك لبعد في المشيّة أما إني سائلك عن ثلاث لا يجعل الله لك في شيء منها مخرجا: أخبرني أخلق الله العباد كما شاء أو كما شاؤوا؟! فقال: كما شاء، قال عليه السلام: فخلق الله العباد لما شاء أو لما شاؤوا؟! فقال: لما شاء، قال عليه السلام: يأتونه يوم القيامة كما شاء أو كما شاؤوا ؟ قال: يأتونه كما شاء، قال عليه السلام: قم فليس إليك من المشيّة شيء.

١٣ ـ الصادق عليه السلام: ﴿لا جبر ولا تفويض ولكن منزلة بين المنزلتين وهي صحة الخلقة وتخلية السرب والمهلة في الوقت والزاد مثل الرحلة والسبب المهيج للفاعل على فعله .

١٤ ـ حديث من عيون اخبار الرضا ـ الشيخ الصدوق الا اعطيكم في هذا أصلا لا تختلفون فيه ولا يخاصمكم عليه احد الا كسرتموه، قلنا: ان

رأيت ذلك، فقال:

ان الله تعالى لم يطع باكراه، ولم يعص بغلبة، ولم يهمل العباد في ملكه، هو المالك لما ملكهم والقادر على ما اقدرهم عليه، فان ائتمر العباد بطاعته لم يكن الله عنها صادرا، ولا منها مانعا، وان ائتمروا بمعصية فشاء ان يحول بينهم وبين ذلك فعل، وان لم يحل ففعلوا فليس هو الذي ادخلهم فيه ثم قال من يضبط حدود هذا الكلام فقد خصم من خالفه.

١٥ ـ سمعت أبا الحسن علي بن موسى بن جعفر عليه السلام يقول: من قال بالجبر فلا تعطوه من الزكاة ولا تقبلوا له شهادة، إن الله تبارك وتعالى لا يكلّف نفسا إلا وسعها، ولا يحملها فوق طاقتها ولا تكسب كل نفس إلا عليها، ولا تزر وازرة وزر أخرى.

١٦ ـ قال رسول الله صلى الله عليه وآله وسلم: عن الله أروي حديثي: إن الله ـ تبارك وتعالى ـ يقول: يا بن آدم، بمشيتي كنت أنت الذي تشاء لنفسك ما تشاء، وبارادتي كنت أنت الذي تريد لنفسك ما تريد، وبفضل نعمتي عليك قويت على معصيتي، وبعصمتي وعوني وعافيتي أديت الي فرائضي فأنا اولى بحسناتك منك، وأنت اولى بسيئاتك مني، فالخير مني إليك بما اوليت بداء، والشر مني إليك بما جنيت جزاء، وبإحساني إليك، قويت على طاعتي، وبسوء ظنك بي قنطت من رحمتي، فلي الحمد والحجة عليك بالبيان، ولي السبيل عليك بالعصيان، ولك جزاء الخير عندي بالاحسان، لم أدع تحذيرك، ولم آخذك عند عزمك ولم اكلفك فوق طاقتك (طاعتك)، ولم احملك من الأمانة إلا بما قدرت (ما أقررت) به على نفسك رضيت لنفسي منك ما رضيت لنفسك مني.

١٧ ـ وفي الكافي باسناده عن مولينا الصادق عليه السلام قال: أمر الله ولم يشأ، وشاء ولم يأمر: أمر إبليس أن يسجد لآدم وشاء أن لا يسجد ولو شاء لسجد، ونهى آدم عن أكل الشجرة وشاء أن يأكل منها، ولو لم يشأ لم يأكل.

١٨ ـ وباسناده عن أبي الحسن عليه السلام قال:

إن لله إرادتين ومشيتين، إرادة حتم وإرادة عزم، ينهي وهو يشاء ويأمر وهو لا يشاء، أو ما رأيت أنه نهى آدم وزوجته أن يأكلا من الشجرة، وشاء ذلك، ولو لم يشأ أن يأكلا لما غلبت مشيتها مشيّة الله.

١٩ ـ أخبر أمير المؤمنين صلوات الله عليه عباية بن ربعي الأسدي حين سأله عن الاستطاعة التي بها يقوم ويقعد ويفعل، فقال له أمير المؤمنين عليه السلام: سألت عن الاستطاعة تملكها من دون الله أو مع الله فسكت عباية، فقال له أمير المؤمنين عليه السلام: قل يا عباية، قال وما أقول؟ قال عليه السلام: إن قلت: إنك تملكها مع الله قتلتك. وإن قلت: تملكها دون الله قتلتك قال عباية: فما أقول يا أمير المؤمنين؟ قال عليه السلام: تقول إنك تملكها بالله الذي يملكها من دونك، فإن ملكها إياك كان ذلك من عطائه، وإن يسلبكها كان ذلك من بلائه، هو المالك لما ملكك والقادر على ما عليه أقدرك، أما سمعت الناس يسألون الحول والقوة حين يقولون لا حول ولا قوة إلا بالله. قال عباية: وما تأويلها يا أمير المؤمنين؟ قال عليه السلام: لا حول عن معاصي الله إلا بعصمة الله ولا قوة لنا على طاعة الله إلا بعون الله، قال: فوثب عباية فقبل يديه ورجليه.

٢٠ ـ أبي عبد الله عليه السلام، قال: سمعته يقول: إن القضاء والقدر خلقان من خلق الله، والله يزيد في الخلق ما يشاء.

٢١ ـ قال رجل لعلي بن الحسين عليه السلام: جعلني الله فداك أبقدر يصيب الناس ما اصابهم أم بعمل؟ فقال عليه السلام: إن القدر والعمل بمنزلة الروح والجسد، فالروح بغير جسد لا تحس والجسد بغير روح صورة لا حراك بها فإذا اجتمعا قويا وصلحا، كذلك العمل والقدر، فلو لم يكن القدر واقعا على العمل لم يعرف الخالق من المخلوق وكان القدر شيئا لا يحس، ولو لم يكن العمل بموافقة من القدر لم يمض ولم يتم، ولكنهما باجتماعها قويا، ولله فيه العون لعباده الصالحين.

140

٢٢ ـ ألا إن من أجور الناس من رأى جوره عدلا وعدل المهتدي جورا، ألا إن للعبد أربعة أعين: عينان يبصر بهما أمر آخرته، وعينان يبصر بهما أمر دنياه، فإذا أراد الله عزّ وجلّ بعبد خيرا فتح له العينين اللتين في قلبه فأبصر بهما العيب وإذا أراد غير ذلك ترك القلب بما فيه، ثم التفت إلى السائل عن القدر فقال: هذا منه، هذا منه.

جعلت فداك ما تقول في القضاء والقدر؟ قال: أقول: إن الله تبارك وتعالى إذا جمع العباد يوم القيامة سألهم عما عهد إليهم ولم يسألهم عما قضى عليهم.

٢٣ ـ بينا علي بن أبي طالب عليه السلام يعبي الكتائب يوم صفّين ومعاوية مستقبله على فرس له يتأكل تحته تأكّلا وعلي عليه السلام على فرس رسول الله صلى الله عليه وآله وسلم المرتجز، وبيده حربة رسول الله صلى الله عليه وآله وسلم، وهو متقلد سيفه ذو الفقار فقال رجل من أصحابه: احترس يا أمير المؤمنين فإنّا نخشى أن يغتالك هذا الملعون، فقال عليه السلام: لئن قلت ذاك إنه غير مأمون على دينه وإنه لأشقى القاسطين وألعن الخارجين على الأئمة المهتدين، ولكن كفى بالأجل حارسا، ليس أحد من الناس إلا ومعه ملائكة حفظة يحفظونه من أن يتردّى في بئر أو يقع عليه حائط أو يصيبه سوء، فإذا حان أجله خلوا بينه وبين ما يصيبه، وكذلك أنا إذا حان أجلي انبعث أشقاها فخضب هذه من هذا ـ وأشار إلى لحيته ورأسه ـ عهد معهودا ووعدا غير مكذوب.

٢٤ ـ إن أمير المؤمنين عليه السلام عدل من عند حائط مائل إلى حائط آخر، فقيل له: يا أمير المؤمنين أتفر من قضاء الله؟ فقال: أفر من قضاء الله إلى قدر الله عزّ وجلّ.

٢٥ ـ قيل لأمير المؤمنين عليه السلام: ألا نحرسك، قال: حرس كل امرئ أجله.

٢٦ ـ وقيل لأمير المؤمنين عليه السلام لما أراد قتال الخوارج: لو

احترزت يا أمير المؤمنين عليه السلام:

أي يومــي مـــن المــوت أفــر

يـــوم ما قـــدر لا أخشــى الــردى

يــوم لـم يقــدر أم يــوم قـــدر

واذا قـــدر لــم يغــن الحــذر

٢٧ ـ دخل الحسين بن علي (ع) على معاوية فقال له: ما حمل اباك على أن قتل أهل البصرة ثم دار عشيا في طرقهم في ثوبين؟ فقال (ع): حمله على ذلك علمه أن ما أصابه لم يكن ليخطئه، وان ما اخطأه لم يكن ليصيبه.

٢٨ ـ يقول: الأعمال على ثلاثة أحوال: فرائض وفضائل ومعاصي وأما الفرائض فبأمر الله عزّ وجلّ، وبرضاء الله وقضاء الله وتقديره ومشيته وعلمه، وأما الفضائل فليست بأمر الله ولكن برضاء الله وبقضاء الله وبقدر الله وبمشيّته وبعلمه، وأما المعاصي فليست بأمر الله ولكن بقضاء الله وبقدر الله وبمشيّته وبعلمه، ثم يعاقب عليها.

وباسناده عنه عليه السلام قال:

لا يكون شيء في الأرض ولا في السماء إلا بهذه الخصال السبع: بمشيّة، وإرادة، وقدر، وقضاء، وإذن، وكتاب، وأجل.

٢٩ ـ الدنيا كلها جهل إلا مواضع العلم، والعلم كله حجة إلا ما عمل به، والعمل كله رياء إلا ما كان مخلصا، والاخلاص على خطر حتى ينظر العبد بما يختم له.

٣٠ ـ عن الحسن بن علي بن أبي طالب (ع)، أنه سُئِل عن قوله عزّ وجلّ: «انا كل شيءٍ خلقناه بقدر» فقال: يقول عزّ وجلّ: انا كل شيءٍ خلقناه لأهل النار بقدر اعمالهم.

٣١ ـ قال الله جلّ جلاله: من لم يرض بقضائي ولم يؤمن بقدري فليلتمس إلهاً غيري.

٣٢ ـ لا يؤمن أحدكم حتى يؤمن بالقدر خيره وشره وحلوه ومره.

٣٣ ـ عن علي بن الحسين عليه السلام قال: خرجت حتى انتهيت إلى هذا الحائط فاتكيت عليه، فإذا رجل عليه ثوبان أبيضان ينظر في وجهي، ثم قال لي: يا علي بن الحسين ما لي أراك كئيبا حزينا، أعلى الدنيا حزنك؟ فرزق الله حاضر للبر والفاجر، فقلت: ما على هذا أحزن وإنه لكما تقول، قال: أفعلى الآخرة حزنك؟ فهو وعد صادق يحكم فيه ملك قاهر، قلت: ما على هذا أحزن وإنه لكما تقول، قال: فعلى ما حزنك؟ فقلت: أنا أتخوف من فتنة ابن الزبير فضحك، ثم قال: يا علي بن الحسين هل رأيت أحدا خاف الله تعالى فلم ينجه؟ قلت: لا، قال: يا علي بن الحسين هل رأيت أحدا سأل الله عزّ وجلّ فلم يعطه؟ قلت: لا، قال عليه السلام: ثم نظرت فاذاً ليس قدّامي أحد.

٣٤ ـ ألا تسئلوني ممّ ضحكت؟ قالوا: بلى يارسول الله. قال عجبت للمرء المسلم، إنه ليس من قضاء يقضيه الله عزّ وجلّ له إلا كان خيرا له في عاقبة أمره.

٣٥ ـ قال كان فيما اوحى الله ـ عزّ وجلّ ـ الى موسى عليه السلام أن يا موسى: ما خلقت خلقا أحب إلي من عبدي المؤمن، وإنما ابتليه لما هو خير له، (واعافيه لما هو خير له) وأنا أعلم بما يصلح عليه أمر عبدي، فليصبر على بلائي، وليشكر نعمائي، وليرض بقضائي، اكتبه في الصديقين عندي إذا عمل برضواني وأطاع أمري.

٣٦ ـ عن أبي جعفر محمد بن عليّ الباقر (ع) قال: إنَّ موسى بن عمران (ع) قال: يارب رضيت بما قضيت، تميت الكبير وتبقي الصغير، فقال الله جلّ جلاله: يا موسى أما ترضاني لهم رازقاً وكفيلاً؟ قال: بلى يارب، فنعم الوكيل أنت ونعم الكفيل.

٣٧ ـ عن الصادق جعفر بن محمد (ع) أنه جاء إليه رجل فقال له: بأبي أنت وأمي عظني موعظة، فقال عليه السلام: إن كان الله تبارك وتعالى قد تكفل بالرزق فاهتمامك لماذا، وإن كان الرزق مقسوما فالحرص لماذا، وإن كان الحساب حقا فالجمع لماذا، وإن كان الخلف من الله عزّ وجلّ حقا فالبخل لماذا، وإن كانت العقوبة من الله عزّ وجلّ النار فالمعصية لماذا، وإن كان الموت حقا فالفرح لماذا، وإن كان العرض على الله عزّ وجلّ حقا فالمكر لماذا، وإن كان الشيطان عدوا فالغفلة لماذا، وإن كان الممر على الصراط حقا فالعجب لماذا، وإن كان كل شيء بقضاء وقدر فالحزن لماذا، وإن كانت الدنيا فانية فالطمأنينة إليها لماذا؟!

٣٨ ـ عن علي بن أبي طالب عليه السلام عن النبي صلى الله عليه وآله وسلم أنه قال: يا علي إن اليقين أن لا ترضى أحدا على سخط الله، ولا تحمدن أحدا على ما آتاك الله، ولا تذمن أحدا على ما لم يؤتك الله، فإن الرزق لا يجره حرص حريص ولا يصرفه كره كاره، فان الله عزّ وجلّ بحكمته وفضله جعل الروح والفرح في اليقين والرضا، وجعل الهمَّ والحزن في الشك والسخط، إنه لا فقر أشد من الجهل ولا مال أعود من العقل، ولا وحدة أوحش من العجب، ولا مظاهرة أوثق من المشاورة، ولا عقل كالتدبير، ولا ورع كالكف عن المحارم، ولا حسب كحسن الخلق، ولا عبادة كالتفكر، وآفة الحديث الكذب، وآفة العلم النسيان، وآفة العبادة الفترة، وآفة الظرف الصلف، وآفة الشجاعة البغي، وآفة السماحة المنّ، وآفة الجمال الخيلاء، وآفة الحسب الفخر.

٣٩ ـ سمعت رسول الله صلى الله عليه وآله وسلم يقول: قدَّر الله المقادير قبل أن يخلق السماوات والأرض بخمسين ألف سنة.

٤٠ ـ وبإسناده عن العالم (ع) [لما سئل: كيف علم الله؟] قال: عَلِمَ، وشاءَ، وأرادَ، وقدَّرَ، وقَضىٰ، وأبدا، فأمضىٰ ما قضىٰ وقضىٰ ما قدَّر، وقدَّر ما أراد، فبعِلمِه كانت المشيّة، وبمشيّته كانت الإرادة، وبإرادته كان

144

التقدير، وبتقديره كان القضاء، وبقضائه كان الإمضاء، فالعلم متقدّم، والمشيّةَ، والمشيّة ثانية، والارادة ثالثة، والتقدير واقع على القضاء بالإمضاء.

٤١ ـ رُوي أنه جاء سراقة بن مالك الى النبي (ص)، فقال: يا رسول الله، بيّن لنا ديننا كأنّا خلقنا الآن، ففيمَ العمل اليوم؟ فيها جفّت به الأقلام، وجرت به المقادير؟ أم فيها يستقبل؟ قال: ففيمَ العمل؟ قال: إعملوا، فكلّ ميسّر لما خُلق له، وكلّ عامل بعمله.

٤٢ ـ وسئل النبي (ص): أنحن في أمر فرغ منه أو أمر مستأنف؟ قال: في أمر فرغ منه، وفي أمر مستأنف.

٤٣ ـ كان أمير المؤمنين (ع) كثيراً ما يقول: إعلموا علماً يقينيّاً أنّ الله ـ تعالى ـ لم يجعل للعبد وإن اشتدّ جهده، وعظمت حيلته، وكثرت مكابدته أن يسبق ما سُمّى له في الذكر الحكيم، ولم يحل بين العبد في ضعفه وقلّه حيلته أن يبلغ ما سُمّى له في الذكر الحكيم.

٤٤ ـ وعن النبي (ص) اعلم: أنّ الأمّة لو اجتمعت على أن ينفعوك بشيءٍ لم ينفعوك إلّا بشيء كتبه الله لك، ولو اجتمعوا على أن يضرّوك، لم يضرّوك إلّا بشيء كتبه الله عليك، رُفعت الأقلام وجفّت الصُحف.

٤٥ ـ أتوا الحسن بن عليّ بعد وفاة عليّ (ع) ليبايعوه فقال: الحمد لله على ما قضى من أمر، وخصَّ من فضل، وعمَّ من أمر، وجلّل من عافية حمدا يتمّم به علينا نعمه ونستوجب به رضوانه، إن الدُنيا دار بلاء وفتنة وكل ما فيها الى زوال، وقد نبأنا الله عنها كيها نعتبر، فقدم إلينا بالوعيد كي لا يكون لنا حجة بعد الانذار، فازهدوا فيها يفنى، وارغبوا فيها يبقى، وخافوا الله في السر والعلانية، إن عليا عليه السلام في المحيا والممات والمبعث عاش بقدر ومات بأجل، وأني ابايعكم على ان تسالموا من سالمت وتحاربوا من حاربت،

٤٦ ـ دخل رجل من أهل العراق على أمير المؤمنين عليه السلام

فقال: أخبرنا عن خروجنا إلى أهل الشام ابقضاء من الله وقدر؟ فقال له أمير المؤمنين عليه السلام: أجل يا شيخ، فوالله ما علوتم تلعة ولا هبطتم بطن واد إلا بقضاء من الله وقدر فقال الشيخ: عند الله أحتسب عنائي يا أمير المؤمنين، فقال: مهلا يا شيخ، لعلك تظن قضاء حتما وقدرا لازما لو كان كذلك لبطل الثواب والعقاب والأمر والنهي والزجر، ولسقط معنى الوعيد والوعد، ولم يكن على مسيء لائمة ولا لمحسن محمدة، ولكان المحسن أولى باللائمة من المذنب والمذنب أولى بالاحسان من المحسن تلك مقالة عبدة الاوثان وخصماء الرحمن وقدرية هذه الأمة ومجوسها، يا شيخ إن الله عزّ وجلّ كلف تخييرا، ونهى تحذيرا، وأعطى على القليل كثيرا، ولم يعص مغلوبا، ولم يطع مكرها ولم يخلق السموات والأرض وما بينها باطلا ذلك ظن الذين كفروا فويل للذين كفروا من النار.

«أنـت الامام الـذي نرجو بطاعته

يـوم النّجاة مـن الرّحـمن غفراناً»

«أوضحت من ديننا ما كان ملتبسا

جــزاك ربـك عـنا فـيه إحساناً»

٤٧ ـ قال أمير المؤمنين عليه السلام في القدر: ألا إنَّ القدر سرٌّ من سرّ الله، وستر من ستر الله، وحرز من حرز الله، مرفوع في حجاب الله، مطويٌّ عن خلق الله، مختوم بخاتم الله، سابق في علم الله، وضع الله العباد عن علمه ورفعه فوق شهاداتهم ومبلغ عقولهم لأنّهم لا ينالونه بحقيقة الرّبانيّة ولا بقدرة الصَّمدانيّة ولا بعظمة النورانيّة ولا بعزّة الوحدانيّة، لأنّه بحر زاخر خالص لله تعالى، عمقه ما بين السماء والأرض، عرضه ما بين المشرق والمغرب، أسود كاللّيل الدّامس، كثير الحيّات والحيتان، يعلو مرّة ويسفل أُخرى، في قعره شمس تضيء لا ينبغي أن يطلع إليها إلّا الله الواحد الفرد، فمن تطلّع إليها فقد ضادَّ الله عزّ وجلّ في حكمه ونازعه في سلطانه، وكشف عن ستره وسرِّه، وباء بغضب من الله ومأواه جهنم وبئس المصير.

٤٨ ـ عن أبي عبد الله (ع) قال: من يموت بالذنوب أكثر مّمن يموت بالآجال، ومن يعيش بالإحسان أكثر مّمن يعيش بالأعمار.

٤٩ ـ رُوي في التوحيد باسناده عن النبي (ص): عن جبرئيل عن الله تبارك وتعالى انه قال: مَنْ أهانَ لي وليًا فقد بارزني بالمحاربة وما ترددتُ في شيءٍ أنا فاعله ما ترددتُ في قبض نفس المؤمن يكره الموت، واكره مساءته ولا بّد له منه.

٥٠ ـ قال رسول الله (ص):

«النّاس معادن، كمعادِن الذهب والفضّة، خيارهم في الجّاهلية خيارهم في الأسلام»

٥١ ـ «ما كُنتَ في ثبوتِكَ ظَهرْتَ بهِ في وجُودِكَ، فليسَ للحقِّ الّا إفاضة الوجود عليك، والحكم لكَ عليك، فلا تَحْمَدْ الّا نفْسَك، ولا تذم الا نفسك، وما يبقىٰ للحقّ إلّا حَمْدَ إضافةِ الوجود، لأنَّ ذلِك لَهُ لَكْ»

وإن من عبادي المؤمنين لمن لا يصلح ايمانه إلا بالفقر ـ ولو اغنيته لافسده ـ وإن من عبادي المؤمنين لمن لا يصلح ايمانه إلا بالغناء ـ ولو افقرته لافسده ذلك ـ وإن من عبادي المؤمنين لمن لا يصلح ايمانه إلا بالسقم ـ ولو صححت جسده لأفسده ذلك ـ وإن من عبادي المؤمنين لمن لا يصلح ايمانه إلا بالصحة ـ ولو اسقمته لافسده ذلك ـ وإني أدلل عبادي بعلمي بقلوبهم، فاني عليم خبير.